PG 10 "WASTE DOES NOT EQUAL PEOPLE"

38 "DIALOGUE ... NOT ... BROADCAST"

{ 59 VCRSP ← ENABLERS } V=VISION IN BOTH ASPECTS
{ 61 VIRAL ← "PROCESS" }

75 FORM OF WASTE: "OVERBURDEN OF INITIATIVES"
∴ ORGANIZATIONAL WASTE

89 CUSTOMIZE HOW "LEAN ADVANCED" IS TRAINED & CERTIFIED,
BASED ON PEOPLE'S ROLES IN THE ORG'N

93 DISCIPLINE BRINGS SIMPLICITY

LEADING WITH LEAN

An Experience-Based Guide to Leading a Lean Transformation

Philip Holt

vakmedianet

"Philip has written a clear and practical guide for Lean champions and existing Lean leaders, which provides an end-to-end guide on designing and sustaining a Lean transformation. If you are looking to build a culture of continuous improvement, whether at one or a multi-site level, this provides some real gems of practical 'know why' and 'know how' for Lean leaders everywhere."

– Jon Tudor, president of the Association for Manufacturing Excellence UK

"In *Leading with Lean*, Philip Holt has ably mapped out the benefits, challenges and effective approaches for leading a Lean transformation. *Leading with Lean* draws on lessons that the author learned from the trenches through to the executive level, while helping to guide a decade-long Lean journey at a global multinational corporation. The book will appeal both to the executive searching for a comprehensive framework for leading with Lean, and to the Lean expert who must speak a common language to gain buy-in and behavior change from the leaders in their organization. Packed with practical wisdom, the reader will no doubt be compelled to put the book down and take action many times before turning the final page."

– Jon Miller, partner at the Gemba Academy

"Philip Holt provides the reader with more than an in depth look at leading with lean, he provides a process along with insightful new concepts to grab the reader and bring them many revelations on leading the lean journey. Concepts such as Leadership Activism, Mosquito leadership, and many others provide a straight forward and practical understanding of leading a lean journey. If you are leading a lean transformation, it is a must read for your leadership team."

– Kevin J. Duggan, President of Duggan Associates

"Although Lean has been around for some time, it continues to make defining inroads both in new industries and in office environments. I can't think of anybody better placed than Philip to share his reflections and experiences accumulated over more than 25 years leading change with Lean in both manufacturing and services. I recommend this book to all, as its practical insights will help us to lead the change we want to see."

– Mathieu Verger, Head of Accounting Operations, Philips Lighting

Philip Holt

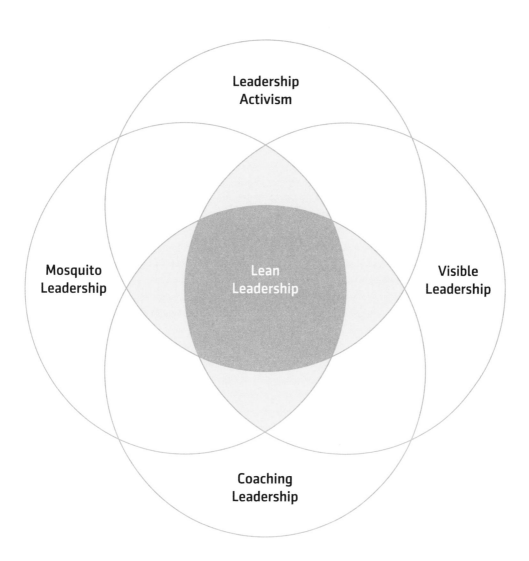

LEADING WITH LEAN
An Experience-Based Guide to Leading a Lean Transformation

COLOFON

Cover design: www.douwehoendervanger.nl

Book design: Jorine Zegwaard, Jorine.biz

Illustrations pages 73, 76, 117, 165, 168 and 178: Studio Wiegers

Editor: Anna Asbury

© Vakmedianet, 2016

Published by Vakmedianet, Deventer, the Netherlands

www.vakmedianet.nl

www.managementimpact.nl

ISBN 978 94 627 6144 5

Printed in the Netherlands

TABLE OF CONTENT

PART V - LEADING WITH LEAN 209

1. INTRODUCTION

The metaphor of the lone violinist

In 2007 the *Washington Post* undertook an experiment,[1] where they asked one of the world's most famous violinists, Joshua Bell, to play at a Washington metro station, the L'Enfant Plaza Station. Just three days earlier he had played to a sell-out audience at Boston's Symphony Hall and even mid-range tickets for his performance had sold for at least $100 per ticket.

On this particular day Joshua played some of his most celebrated pieces, over a period of 45 minutes, as more than 1,000 commuters passed him by, yet only seven people stopped to listen for even a minute (the maximum was three minutes) and only 27 gave money. Everyone else was simply too busy to stop. Outside of the context of his usual performing environment, he was not recognised and his talent unappreciated. He earned just $37.

When we look at what happened in this situation, it is easy to dismiss this as due to the busy lives and tight schedules of the many commuters who passed by Joshua that day. However, if his performance had been publicised in some way, and general knowledge had got around that he was playing there that morning, I'm certain that a crowd would have formed and that people would have taken the time to listen to his performance. In fact, what I believe happened is that no-one recognised the quality of the artist available to enhance their morning commute and to provide them with a boost to their daily wellbeing. Had they known who the performer was, and the world-class status that he carries, I'm positive that many of them would have stopped, accepting the short-term impact on their schedule to benefit from the cultural enrichment on offer, along with the 'bragging rights' around the water cooler later that day. However, with the exception of the few who stopped for a fleeting moment, the vast majority were unwilling to take the risk of stopping and interfering with their schedules, even if this might have provided them with a very tangible benefit.

When we look at the experiment from that perspective, we could easily be critical of the people who failed to stop, suggesting that, if only they would look around in the world occasionally, they could have enhanced their lives by taking advantage of an opportunity to experience the music of an expert violinist. However, in the article there were two quotes that can provide us with an alternative perspective:

If a great musician plays great music but no one hears...
was he really any good?
- Gene Weingarten, the author of the article

At the beginning I was just concentrating on playing the music.
I wasn't really watching what was happening around me...
- Joshua Bell

Linking this article to the purpose of this book, it has, for me, become a metaphor for being a Leader of Lean Transformation, in that it can sometimes feel like you are this lone violinist, an expert (as far as anyone can claim to be) in the field of Lean Thinking, perhaps able to provide the organisation with a new way of working, providing the opportunity to become world-class but with everyone too busy to listen.

However, just as with Joshua Bell and the *Washington Post's* experiment, if you have not established the context and a compelling reason for the 'audience' to listen to you, then your organisation will continue with their daily business regardless and you will remain unheard. If you simply concentrate on playing your tunes: running Kaizen events, Lean projects, training courses, etc., without observing what is happening around you, it is likely that you'll be oblivious to the lack of real change that is occurring, until it's unfortunately too late.

The original lone violinist

Taiichi Ohno

On 29 February 1912, a child was born who would become one of the world's least well known revolutionaries. That child was Taiichi Ohno and, had he revolutionised medicine, communication technology or the arts, he would most likely have been far better known than he is today.

However, Ohno-san revolutionised first the Toyota Motor Corporation and then, as a result of the success they achieved through the system he developed, the whole automotive industry and subsequently industry as a whole. As a result, he has a very respectable esoteric recognition but it is much more modest than I believe that it ought to be.

Nevertheless, for those of us for whom excellence through Lean Thinking is admired, Ohno-san embodied the traits that the Lean Leader must have in order to be successful:

- Respect for people
- Integrity
- Discipline
- Purpose
- Stamina
- Humility

There are many stories about Taiichi Ohno and he is generally credited with the creation of 'Ohno Circles' and of establishing '5 x Why' within the culture of Toyota. However, one of my favourites is about his influence on the development of SMED (single minute exchange of dies).[2]

Impossibility leads to new ideas

In the 1960s, Toyota's changeover times for their 1,000-tonne press machines was between two and four hours and whenever a changeover took place the entire line had to stop, which led to lower production. At the time, Volkswagen was performing their changeovers in less than two hours, so Toyota set the goal of doing the same and, with the help of Shigeo Shingo, they were able to reduce changeover time from four hours to one hour.

Despite this incredible improvement in changeover time, Taiichi Ohno said the following:

Now reduce the changeover time to less than 10 minutes!

Shigeo Shingo and the team thought that challenge was impossible but, since they were all sufficiently intimidated by the determination of Taiichi Ohno, they went about trying to meet the challenge.

A concept that came out of this challenge was to attempt to transition all internal changeover time into external changeover time, leading to several innovations in the preparation and execution of changeover and, after some trials, experimentation and testing, the team was able to reduce the changeover time to seven minutes, then from seven minutes to three minutes.

According to Wakamatsu, this challenge and the team's response led to two critical aspects of the Toyota production system:

1. Single-minute exchange of die (SMED)
2. One-piece flow

Ohno-san was determined that breakthrough thinking was required in order that Toyota could not only match their competitors' changeover times but could smash through them and take a competitive advantage. To do this he had to play the lone violinist in his belief and commitment to this cause but, unlike in the *Washington Post* experiment, he could not play the tune on his own and instead had to engage with the Team and utilise their knowledge, skills and expertise to achieve the goal. They understood the purpose, respected his authority to challenge the status quo and, together, delivered a world-class performance. The lone violinist started to form an orchestra.

Being heard

It should now be clear that whilst the Lean Transformation Leader should be a lone violinist in terms of their unconventional view and challenge to the status quo, the ability to be heard must be inherent in the approach they take.

For the Lean Leader, communication is an essential part of the Lean Transformation effort and they will make every effort to ensure that the organisation's people are aware of their existence, the reasons for the initiative, its objectives, the plan, opportunities, expected contribution and progress on an ongoing basis.

Being heard has to be a key element of the Lean Transformation yet, as with any good communication strategy, the important element of being heard is listening.

> *When you talk, you are only repeating what you already know.*
> *But if you listen, you may learn something new.*
> - Dalai Lama

(handwritten annotations at top of page)
✗ - LISTEN TO ID NEEDS
- DIFFERENTIATE FROM "WANTS"
↳ CHALLENGE - HELPING ORG'NS DIFFERENTIATE

It is therefore essential that the Lean Leader listens intently to what the organisation needs, the 'voice of the customer', for their efforts, while being careful not to confuse what the organisation says it wants with what it needs. This subtle but important difference will be one of the critical success factors for the Lean Leader, as the organisation will not know what it doesn't know. This is a common error for the Lean Leader, attempting to please the organisation by giving it what it asks for instead of what it needs. The analogy for this is the difference between a shopkeeper and a doctor; as the shopkeeper provides customers with what they ask for (within legal limits of course), while the doctor listens to the symptoms of the customer (the patient) and attempts to understand the underlying root cause before providing a course of treatment. The Lean Transformation Leader must therefore act as the doctor, not the shopkeeper.

Why Leading with Lean?

Across the world employees are disengaged and this is recognised as a problem at the senior-leadership level across industry around the world. According to Gallup's Global Employee Engagement Survey[3] only 13% of employees worldwide are engaged at work. Even more concerning is the revelation that 24% are 'actively disengaged', meaning that they are unhappy and unproductive at work and liable to spread negativity amongst their colleagues. Furthermore, according to a report by the Harvard Business Review Analytic Services,[4] based on responses mainly from senior executives, 71% of respondents rank employee engagement as very important to achieving overall organisational success.

This gulf between the state of employee engagement, which is without exception across industries and cultures, and the recognition by senior leadership of its necessity to drive performance, should be a major concern for any organisation's leadership and its resolution the most significant executive priority. Therefore, a key proposition of this book is that an organisation's leadership makes the difference between engaged and disengaged people and between a culture of high or mediocre performance and that Lean Leadership is the most effective methodology to achieve high levels of employee engagement, a high-performance organisation and ultimately a quality mindset.

To attain the state of Lean Leadership, four complementary leadership styles must be practised, as described in the book, with the intent that they will result in an organisation focussed on people so as to engage them in their work:

1. Leadership Activism
2. Visible Leadership
3. Mosquito Leadership
4. Coaching Leadership

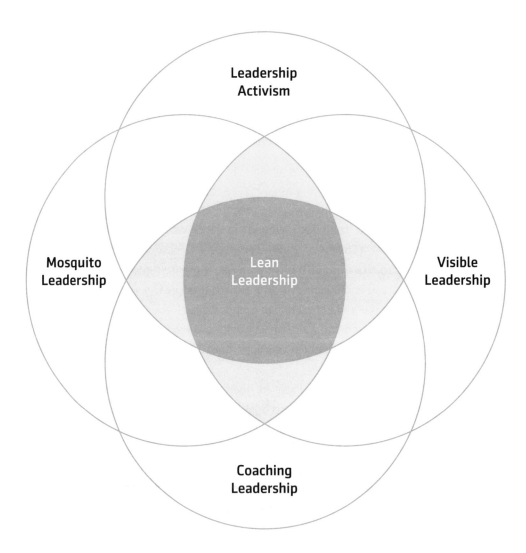

The Leading with Lean Venn diagram

These leadership styles, when lived authentically, will give the leader the ability to connect with their team members and transform the behaviours, mindset and culture of their organisation.

This is not to say that these styles can be forced or easily mastered. It will take a real commitment from each leader to adopt Lean Leadership and the styles required to make it successful but, even in the early days of their adoption, an immediate difference will be seen, provided that the leader is willing to move into a state of conscious incompetence (admitting what they don't yet know) and having the humility to make mistakes and learn.

The long-term return will be significant for both the individual and the organisation and, in the author's organisation, Royal Philips, several years of Lean Transformation have demonstrated significant improvements in leadership and business performance for those areas of the business that have truly seized the opportunity.

What's in it for you?

Being a Lean Transformation Leader is a challenging job and the risk-reward ratio is not always obviously positive in comparison to taking a 'regular job'. However, for those who are successful, the opportunity to make an impact far beyond what could ordinarily be achieved as a sole contributor is huge, and the insight, understanding and learning that can be gained, extensive.

[handwritten margin note: NOT FOR THE 'FAINT OF HEART']

As a result, the career opportunities for those Lean Leaders who make it work are significant, normally leading to leadership positions across a wide range of functions and on a global basis. Be in no doubt about it, Lean Leaders who are successful will receive multiple offers for attractive roles and will experience a career that will be the envy of many of their family, friends and colleagues.

Nevertheless, I have personally found that the most attractive attributes have always been the learning and the camaraderie that is derived from the Transformation and the many Kaizen events, coaching sessions, Kaikaku experiences and training sessions that you are involved in will allow you to touch the professional lives of many people and learn a great deal about yourself.

A particularly fulfilling element of Lean Leadership is the training and coaching of colleagues from across the hierarchical spectrum of the organisation. I will go into more detail later in the book about the importance of the certification process in establishing a core competency in Lean Thinking but for the moment it is suffice to say that both training and coaching are of equal importance and a Lean Leader will be involved in both to ensure that knowledge transfer and practical elements of learning are supported.

[handwritten note: — MAKE 'CERTIFICATION' REAL]
[handwritten note: — TAKES LEARNING/PRACTICE ITERATIVELY]

One of the most exciting and unusual aspects of the role of a Lean Leader is the opportunity to coach senior leaders and executives within the organisation. In fact, this is one of the few areas where I have observed more junior members of the organisation coaching more senior members, in contrast with the usual situation whereby executive coaches are 'bought in' from external parties. This provides a unique symbiotic relationship, where the Lean Leader can coach the executive in a different way of thinking, problem solving and behaving, whilst the executive can educate the Lean Leader in some of the specific strategic challenges for the organisation. This is not easy for the Lean Leader and provides another challenge which a 'regular job' would not, but for the right person this is another reason to embrace being a 'lone violinist'.

Given the multitude of challenges and the unique nature of the role, there is no doubt that it is a tough job and that it takes a special kind of person to do it successfully but, for those who master it, it is one of the most rewarding and interesting roles that you can have in the organisation.

Understanding value in the eyes of the customer

Womack and Jones codified Lean Thinking in their book of the same name5 The first step is to define value in the eyes of the customer. I believe that writing a book demands the same approach, so I discussed with a number of potential customers and colleagues what they wanted from a book about Lean Thinking. The answer was a 'how to' manual that would combine some practical examples of how Lean can be applied, with clear guidance on how to transform an organisation, with particular emphasis on the role of the Lean Transformation Leader.

Surveying the broad landscape of Lean books on offer, I identified that there was a gap in the market to address their needs. Having a personal desire to share my experience in this field, I decided to embark on the journey of bringing it into print. The result is, I hope, a guide for the Lean Transformation Leader who really wants to do more than simply apply the Lean tools and run Kaizen events. While these activities are important, true transformation of an organisation results from a meaningful intervention in the behaviour of its employees at every level and particularly at the leadership level.

The purpose of this book is therefore to provide the Lean Leaders out there (either currently practising or aspiring) with some guidance and support in ensuring that the organisation hears their tune and recognises the opportunity that a new way of thinking and working will bring to the business performance. Within this book you will find guidance on how to do this step by step as you navigate the long Lean Transformation journey ahead of you, whether you are right at the start of it, or a few years in.

Structure of the book

The structure of this book is intended to guide you, the Lean Transformation Leader, through your personal journey navigating your personal change curve and the frustrations, challenges and successes that it will bring. Whether you are responsible for the Lean Transformation of a global corporation, are the CEO, a head of department or the Lean champion of a single site, I hope this book will guide you in doing the right things and reassure you that you will succeed if you maintain the integrity of your approach. While this book is intended to be read by people at various levels in the organisation and in different types of organisation, all readers should have a very similar aim, to transform, to the extent that they are able, the way that their organisation operates, using Lean Thinking as the means to achieve this change.

The book is based upon my own experiences Leading with Lean in a global organisation as well as my observations from researching and visiting many organisations at various stages in their Lean Transformations. With this book I aim to bring that experience together in one place. I have made the decision to focus on the Leadership aspect of Lean Thinking, so please forgive me for explaining the Lean Tools only at the conceptual level, where further detail would have made the book far too long. I have provided notes for most, if not all, of the references, which should provide you with any additional information that you may need.

At the end of every chapter there is a blank page for your reflections but in a way that in Lean Thinking is called 'Hansei'.[6] Hansei is an opportunity for reflecting back on one's self, or one's own action, and therefore provides the reader with a few moments to think about how what they have just read links to their own way of working and actions. I would therefore encourage you to take a pen and write down your thoughts at the end of each chapter before reading further.

When it comes to your own way of working, what are:

1. Your key learning points?
2. The changes that you could make?
3. Current problems that they would help to solve?

By doing this at the end of every chapter, you will hopefully already be practising a key element of Lean Leadership, which is covered in more detail later in the book.

Whilst the book may be constantly used as a reference manual throughout your Lean Transformation, it is essential that you ensure that the journey follows the advice in full, as skipping over elements of it, especially because they are difficult or you don't feel that they are relevant to you or your organisation, will sow the seeds of failure.

Very few organisations have sustainably achieved Lean Excellence and the reason is that it is hard to do, requiring discipline and at least one lone violinist to succeed. The intention is that, with this book by your side, you can lead your organisation in joining that elite club of world-class enterprises and derive the benefits that it brings.

The sequencing of the book was challenging to decide upon, as many aspects of a Lean Transformation and a Lean Management System are interdependent and non-sequential. However, for convenience I have arranged them in what I believe is a rational order:

Part I - *Planning to Lead*

Understanding why your organisation needs to undertake a Lean Transformation is critical to its long-term success. In the first part of the book I explain how to establish this, plan the Lean Transformation and get started on the journey. Key elements of this are understanding the different levels of Lean, its principles and what Lean Leadership means.

In this initial section you will also learn how change and communication planning is essential throughout the journey and the challenges and opportunities that exist in building Lean expertise. This includes discovering to what degree unconscious incompetence is getting in your organisation's way and overcoming it.

Finally I will take you through the building of your Transformation Model, with some practical examples of how to build a model that will deliver long-term Lean transformation and operational excellence.

Part II - *Learning to Lead*

In the second part of the book the first two requirements for Lean Leadership, Leadership Activism and Visible Leadership, are covered. This requires that we learn to lead. To begin this experimentation, we first need to understand, plan, communicate and execute our business strategy, so we first spend a chapter on Hoshin Kanri, a methodology for doing just that.

Further to this I explain how Leadership Activism harnesses a leader's commitment to the change in an effective way, how they can encourage and create more activist leaders in their organisation, and how discipline, rather than stifling creativity and dampening enthusiasm, can be utilised to create competitive advantage and free up time for innovation.

Finally, I explain how Visible Leadership is integral to the leader and their team members' learning Lean Leadership and how operational excellence will transform their business performance.

1. DESIGN THE PATH
2. BUILD THE PATH
3. THEN START TO TRVEL THE PATH
4. ADJUST AS WE LEARN & GROW

Part III - **Leading at Scale**

Once we have learnt how Leading with Lean and Lean Thinking will transform our business, it is important to scale the impact across the whole organisation and in this part of the book I discuss how the leader and the organisation may learn from both their own and others' successes and use this learning to avoid reinventing the wheel.

The final two elements of Lean Leadership, Mosquito Leadership and Coaching Leadership, are also introduced. The first of these is sometimes controversial, as a mosquito may seem like a peculiar animal for a leadership metaphor, until you consider that the term 'viral marketing' or the concept of spreading ideas virally are accepted vernacular in business and social circles, despite the fact that none of us would want to actually contract a virus. I would therefore ask that you keep an open mind when it comes to the concept of Mosquito Leadership, as it is one that I consider extremely important to the success of a Lean Transformation and to Lean Leadership.

In the second half of this part of the book, the concepts of Coaching Leadership and the business excellence competition are introduced, both providing the education in Lean Thinking that is required for the entire organisation.

Part IV - **Leading Excellence**

Having taken the reader through the critical concepts of Leading with Lean, in Part IV of the book I establish how the leader can take the organisation through the transformation by putting their Lean Leadership into practice. This involves creating the fundamentals of a Lean Enterprise that will allow you to break the mediocrity barrier and deliver the operational excellence that we require.

To do this, you will need to make your business excellence team's approach excellent, so I've discussed how to achieve this effective, model set-up and, lastly, demonstrated how we must reconcile the age-old dichotomy of the value stream versus local autonomy.

Part V - **Leading with Lean**

In the final section of the book the reader will learn how to make the new way of working the culture of their organisation and how doing so is not a single, continuous journey but a lifetime of journeys. I will describe how this requires the leader to have significant stamina, as the transformation will span many years and require a long-term resolve which many lack the ability or motivation to maintain.

The book culminates by summarising the elements required to Lead with Lean and the mindset of excellence required to attain all elements of the Lean Leadership Model.

YIN/YANG OF EMPOWERMENT & CONTROL

" LEAN (HAPPINESS) ISN'T A DESTINATION — IT's THE SHOES YOU PUT ON IN THE MORNING "

I hope that you not only enjoy this book but that it provides you with inspiration to develop your own Leadership further and perhaps to break through some of the barriers that you may have met in your attempts to transform your organisation.

HANSEI

Before moving onto the next chapter, please take a few moments to reflect. When it comes to your own way of working, what are:

1. Your key learning points?

NEEDS vs WANTS
4 TYPES OF LEADERSHIP FOR LEAN
NOT FOR 'FAINT OF HEART'
∞ JOURNEY

2. The changes that you could make?

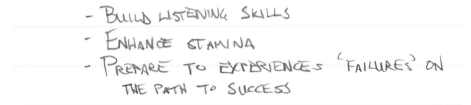

- BUILD LISTENING SKILLS
- ENHANCE STAMINA
- PREPARE TO EXPERIENCES 'FAILURES' ON THE PATH TO SUCCESS

3. Current problems that they would help to solve?

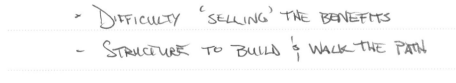

- DIFFICULTY 'SELLING' THE BENEFITS
- STRUCTURE TO BUILD & WALK THE PATH

PART I

PLANNING TO LEAD

Lean = ?? ?? ?? ?

ANALOGOUS TO DEFINING 6σs

STAT → 1 PPB (3.4 PPM)

↑

DMAIC ++

↑

DEMING / JURAN / · · ·

2. WHAT IS LEAN?

The different levels of Lean

The question 'What is Lean?' is one which I believe will be argued and debated until the end of time and I will therefore avoid being perceived as arrogant in trying to settle the debate and will instead, humbly, offer a model answer that I have developed throughout my years of practice and which has served me well.

The first thing to say is that the word Lean works at three levels, as embodied in the Shingo Levels of Transformation:[1]

SHINGO LEVELS OF TRANSFORMATION
PRINCIPLE-DRIVEN
SYSTEM-DRIVEN
TOOL-DRIVEN

The Shingo Institute Levels of Transformation

These three levels, in part, explain why the word Lean has different meanings to different people and organisations and it is therefore imperative that before beginning a Lean Transformation you establish what Lean should mean to your organisation and its people. Assuming that everyone will understand the meaning in the same way is the first step on the path to failure and therefore significant time should be invested in this effort. In my experience, the only meaning that Lean can have, if you are to transform your organisation into one that is truly world-class, is one of Lean Thinking, a principle-driven approach that embeds the Lean Principles into the very culture of the organisation. Within this definition, the Lean and Six-Sigma Toolkits will be utilised as required, and appropriate systems will be put into place to drive improvement of the value streams. Most importantly, however, all Team Members, from those adding value at the 'Gemba' (the shop floor, workshop, operating theatre, call centre, etc.) to the team leaders, supervisors, area managers, middle managers, directors and executives, will be trained, coached and certified in the Lean Principles, embedding them into their way of working and, ultimately, the culture of the organisation.

LEAN as an acronym

I have therefore developed the word lean into an acronym, one which I think adequately articulates the essence of what the Lean Leader should see as the purpose of Lean, and it came to me while I was using an alternative acronym as a provocative but fun way of describing to a class precisely what Lean is not. Some of you may already know the alternative acronym which is:

"WE WERE 5S'ed"
"$5B SAVINGS"

LEAN = Less Employees Are Needed

I often use this acronym to deal with one of the symptoms of the abuse of Lean over the last few years, which is the perception by many people, especially those most vulnerable to the misapplication of Lean, that it is a management tool to reduce the headcount and to downsize the organisation. However, nothing could be further from the truth in those organisations where Lean has been utilised as a strategy to enable the business to attain world-class excellence.

STRYKER

Lean will certainly result in achieving more with the same resources, as its primary intent is to remove the waste in the system through attacking the root causes. However, where a principle-driven approach is taken, waste does not equal people. On the contrary, people are viewed as the only asset that appreciates in value over time, as we are capable of learning, adapting and adding additional value through the removal of waste in the value stream.

Explaining the difference between removing waste and reducing the headcount is always a challenge and the more cynical of colleagues can assume that it is simply a case of semantics. However, Collin McCloughlin, of Enna.com, stated it very well in his LinkedIn article[2] 'Five myths about lean that are holding you back':

> Lean organizations achieve success by eliminating unnecessary work. Does this mean they eliminate jobs? There is a difference between work and a job: "Work" implies activity, while "job" usually indicates employment. Do you regret that you no longer have to wash clothes by hand? Do you miss sweeping chimneys and turning a crank to get your car to start? I doubt it. Those processes have improved and this allows us all to spend more time doing meaningful work. This is what Lean aims to do for your job. Eliminating unnecessary activity makes employees more

valuable by freeing up time and energy for more important and fulfilling work. Lean is meant to allow us to lead a less burdensome life, to better humanity for all through the work and effort we put into our jobs.

Lean Thinking therefore teaches us that, where we actively apply Principle-Driven Lean Thinking, we will drive customer value up and see the QCD (quality, cost and delivery) performance of the value streams, and hence the organisation, flourish. Where the organisation has unimaginative and traditional leadership, stuck in the status quo, this will result in the organisation requiring fewer people, as they will maintain the status quo in terms of their markets, market share and customer base. However, where Lean Thinking has been truly established, the leadership will understand the full extent of the growth opportunity that has been created and will use this platform to take the organisation into new markets, develop new products or services, find new customers and grow /STRYKER market share.

Thinking Lean

Lean Leaders must therefore enable Lean Thinking within their organisations and the acronym that I have developed to explain how to do this is:

> **LEAN = *leadership, excellence, analysis and no***

- ■ **Leadership:** In Lean Thinking, leadership is not just for those people provided with the job title but for everyone within the organisation to take leadership in their own domain. Through setting the appropriate boundary conditions, taking a people-focussed approach (respect for people) to our business processes and ensuring that everyone is focussed on what the customer / consumer perceives as value, we can utilise daily management to ensure continuous flow (of products, information, knowledge and services) throughout the value stream.

- ■ **Excellence:** The pursuit of excellence is core to Lean and this is enabled through some of the key tenets of a Lean Business System. Utilising small batch sizes, continuous flow, built-in quality and pull systems (not only for products but also information, knowledge and services), all of which have been based upon the customer demand, we enable daily management to drive rapid problem solving and Kaizen. Team members are encouraged to constantly experiment with improvements to the system and through 'Go-to-Gemba' (the place where the value is added) leaders are able to coach and act as teachers.

■ **Analysis:** Lean Thinking has its foundation built on fact based decision making. Through the application of A3 thinking and a short-interval control approach, our people are rapidly involved in problem solving, using the appropriate tools (including both the Lean and Six Sigma toolkit), to find the root cause and implement countermeasures. However, experimentation and learning are a major element and therefore 'at-the-Gemba' problem solving with 'cardboard engineering' experimentation is common and this approach is not just for the shop floor but is applicable all the way to the boardroom.

■ **No:** In my experience the 'secret formula' of Lean Thinking is Hoshin Kanri (or Policy Deployment) and the one area that most organisations struggle to apply. Having the courage to say NO to the multitude of opportunities that an organisation has and to have the laser-like focus required to choose only those few things that will truly provide the breakthrough results is extremely difficult and only a few organisations have the level of discipline and stamina required to truly do this. Without the ability to say no, most businesses tend to overload their people and fail to execute effectively.

[handwritten margin note: "TAKE THE RIGHT" THINGS OFF THE PLATE - NO "CURES FOR WHICH THERE ARE NO KNOWN DISEASES"]

The Lean Principles

Womack and Jones codified Lean Thinking with their five steps:[3]
1. Understand what the customer values.
2. Visualise the value stream and remove the waste.
3. Create flow.
4. So that the customer can pull the value.
5. Continually strive for perfection.

[handwritten margin note: • SOLVE MY PROBLEM COMPLETELY • DON'T WASTE MY TIME • PROVIDE - WHAT I WANT - WHEN I WANT IT - WHERE I WANT IT • MINIMIZE THE # OF DECISIONS I MUST MAKE TO SOLVE MY PROBLEM — "UNIVERSAL V.O.C."]

These Lean Principles are quite well known by a large number of people throughout Industry and there is a general agreement that they exemplify how an organisation can manage its value streams toward operational excellence. Nevertheless, it is a consistent challenge to attain this state due to the difficulty in aligning the organisation around delivering customer value with the minimum of waste, due to a number of endemic disablers . Throughout this book I will attempt to identify these disablers and provide you with the enablers that will ensure that you can take your business on the journey to world-class.

Those organisations that have embedded Lean Thinking into their company culture have demonstrated superior performance over significant periods of time and prove that Lean is, above all, about integrating a principle-driven approach to an organisation's management philosophy.

Lean Leadership

Throughout the Lean Transformation, the lone violinist will need to maintain strong Leadership and to be successful will need to develop a network of Lean Leaders in the organisation, ultimately aiming to make their own role redundant as the leadership style in the business transitions to one that is embedded in Lean Thinking.

There are four interrelated styles of Lean Leadership that will ensure that you are successful in your own, and your coachee's, transformational leadership:

1. **Leadership Activism:** Being an Active Lean Leader, as opposed to an advocate or supporting leader, is critical to success. Anyone can support an initiative for transformation, or advocate it to anyone who will listen, but an activist is in the game, leading through example and action and learning by doing.

2. **Visible Leadership:** Whilst being active in the change, the Lean Leader must also be visible to their teams, running the Kaizen events, coaching and being at the Gemba as often as they can. Planning and communicating from HQ might be comfortable but it will not enthuse the team as it needs to.

3. **Mosquito Leadership:** This form of Lean Leadership is the one that will really infect the organisation and create the viral change that is necessary. The Mosquito Leader will be a form of irritant to the status quo but it is exactly this paradigm-breaking approach that will ensure that the organisation can break the chains of its current culture and make the step change that is necessary.

4. **Coaching Leadership:** The last form of leadership that is required is the one that will engage the Lean Leader most with the organisation. This is the approach that brings them into direct contact with the team members in coaching behavioural change but it is a real challenge, as it requires them to have the patience to 'stay off the field of play' as they let the people best able to make the change do it.

All 4 styles are covered within their own chapters of the book and are equally important to success. Nevertheless, they will require significant self-development and a true belief in the journey of transformation.

Lean is simply good business

I hope this chapter has confirmed what you might already know, that Lean Thinking is relatively simple in essence but requires highly effective leadership to ensure synchronisation of the organisation's thinking.

Lean Leadership starts with the lone violinist but must, virally, through a systematic development of the organisation's people, become the modus operandi of everyone in the business and the way that we deliver the value that our customers demand.

Lean Leadership will only permeate the organisation if there is a reason for it to do so and the Lean Transformation Leader must therefore establish the case for change. In the next chapter I will explore how we may best do this.

HANSEI

Before moving onto the next chapter, please take a few moments to reflect.
When it comes to your own way of working, what are:

1. your key learning points?

"WASTE ≠ PEOPLE" / PEOPLE = GROWTH ASSET

L EADERSHIP
E XCELLENCE
A NALYSIS
No

2. the changes that you could make?

- RESIST TEMPTATION TO MICRO MANAGE
- WALK AWAY FROM MY DESK/LAPTOP/PHONE ...
- ENHANCE HOW THE 4 LEADERSHIP STYLES INTERACT
   → IT'S NOT JUST 4 SEPARATE PARTS

3. current problems that they would help to solve?

"US VS. THEM"

Before I read even the
1st word below the caption
I wrote about the Sinek
video — it had a profound
impact on me!

←

✗ ALSO: "ASK WHY 5 TIMES" IS A
USEFUL TOOL TO BOTH CHALLENGE
AND JUSTIFY WHATEVER WE PROPOSE
AS REASONS FOR EXISTENCE

LENSES OF "4 C's"   ⇒ CONTRIBUTORS?
                       (AS IN TEAM
                        MEMBERS)
        CUSTOMER
        CONUSMER
        COMPETITION   ←
        CAPABILITIES

3. BEGINNING THE CHANGE

Start with Why

[handwritten: SIMON SINEK VIDEO]

Many readers will be familiar with Simon Sinek's 'Start with Why' TED talk[1] and may have read his book of the same name.[2] Simon mentions in his talk that he didn't invent this way of thinking but simply codified it, though I count myself as one of the many people grateful to him for rationalising an approach that was implicitly known but previously difficult to articulate, teach or to set as a standard.

This way of thinking is critical when it comes to establishing the case for change, as before we can determine what needs to change, and how to do so, we need to understand why we exist as an organisation; What is our raison d'être? Why does it matter that we exist?

When we can articulate this well, we can then start to measure our current performance against that vision and this will enable the agreement on why we need to change and allow us to communicate this to all parts of our organisation. Don't underestimate this and do not fall into the trap of rushing this step, determining it in a couple of hours as either your own view, that of the CEO or of the executive sponsor of the Lean Transformation.

[handwritten: NO SHORTCUTS]

Instead, this should be determined in a workshop including the key stakeholders of the organisation. These will differ from one organisation to another, but could include such people as:

- Leadership team / board of management
- Middle management
- Supervisors
- Union officials
- Employee representatives
- Customers

[handwritten: FULL RANGE OF STAKEHOLDERS]

In the workshop the group will align and agree upon the vision and mission of the organisation, the factors that influence its performance. Looking through the lenses of the customer, consumer, competition and their own capabilities, they will create a compelling 'Why' to explain the organisation's existence.

Most importantly, they will do this in a way that gains agreement amongst the key stakeholders. Once this is established, the team will determine the gaps between their

[handwritten: FROM "PIE IN THE SKY" TO TANGIBLE ISSUES]

VERY FEW

current performance and the 'Why', creating a case for change that can both motivate and sustain the organisation in the long journey ahead.

An important element of the capabilities part is the effectiveness of the organisation in engaging and enabling its people. For those of us who subscribe to the theory of Lean Thinking the people of the organisation are the only asset capable of continuously appreciating in value. I say capable as unfortunately not all organisations create the environment for them to do so but, if your transformation is to be successful, this must be a leading part of the strategy. We must therefore ensure that the 'Why' of the organisation, as well as the case for change, is explicit in its explanation of the organisation's expectations of, and commitment to, its people.

All of the above must be done on the basis of fact, determining our customers' and consumers' perceptions through data points, such as NPS (net promoter score),[3] Field Call Rates, relative market share, time-to-market and QCD (quality, cost and delivery) performance in comparison to our competition and an honest calibration of our own functional and technical capabilities.

DEPENDABILITY OF THE DATA CAN BE A CHALLENGE, BUT CAN BE HANDLED IF OUR EYES ARE OPEN

Communication, communication, communication

From the very first day of the transformation communication will be critical to success. To prepare for the workshop in which we will establish the case for change, you should undertake thorough stakeholder analysis[4] to understand who are the right people to include. *RULE OF 9* In the workshop you will also need to enhance the stakeholder map through alignment with the participants and agreement on the level of commitment and influence of the different groups.

While doing this you will ensure that you have sufficiently developed the level of granularity for the stakeholder groups, in some cases working at the individual level, for example with the CEO (chief executive officer) or CFO (chief financial officer), and in some cases more generalised groups (e.g. the product engineering group). The important thing is to ensure that the level of grouping of the people is sufficient to build and execute an effective communication plan (CommPlan).

Better!

As we run the CommPlan through the PDCA Cycle (plan–do–check–act or plan–do–check–adjust)[5] we will continuously learn what resonates with our people. This is intended to create a dialogue with the organisation, not to broadcast to them. Gone are the days of simply posting memos on the notice board, corporate communication emails or large-scale 'Town Hall' meetings. These forms of one-way communication have past their sell-by date and will not provide the learning environment that the organisation needs to be successful in its transformation, nor will they engage the biggest driver of change, the people who make up the organisation.

Instead, a multi-channel two-way conversation is necessary, utilising both traditional face-to-face discussions amongst teams and more modern e-enabled platforms, such as social networks. The balance of the tools used will very much depend on the size and scale of the organisation, with a small, single-site business using in-person communication as a much larger portion of their CommPlan than a large, multisite, multinational organisation, where in-person local communication will be augmented by social platforms, webcasts and intranets to provide the global connectivity and best practice sharing.

In my current organisation, the most successful communication platform used is what is called the Philips Community[6], an enterprise social platform for sharing ideas, information, announcements and best practices, where groups can be formed and joined by any individual in the company. Whilst there is a level of corporate moderation to ensure that the guidelines of acceptable use are followed, it is fairly independent and is populated through user-generated content. Of the many groups that now exist, the *Continuous-Improvement@Philips* group is one of the most successful, with over 2500 members[7] and a constant stream of dialogue between members sharing, asking, answering and talking about their experiences.

This level of attainment of communication was only reached through the development and execution of a solid CommPlan and the utilisation of multi-channel communication across the stakeholder groups. In line with John Kotter's[8] warning of 'declaring victory too soon', even when a high maturity is reached, the PDCA loop must continue if entropy is to be avoided.

An ongoing dialogue with the organisation is critical to our Lean Journey and therefore sustained management of the plan is essential.

Getting on the change curve

John Kotter is well known for his research and teaching in change management, which in more recent times has developed into an updated theory of change leadership. His model on change has detractors and other theories and approaches exist. However, I've found Kotter's change model to be extremely useful and the Lean Transformation Model that I will talk about in Chapter 5 utilises the thinking in the model to take the organisation through its journey of change.

Like all models, it has omissions, as otherwise it would not be a model but would be reality and hence too complicated to apply. My advice is therefore to utilise the model but to ensure that you are learning what works and what doesn't as you progress. The

CommPlan will support this learning and the opportunity to adapt as you go.
The elements of Kotter's model are mentioned throughout the book, with the main coverage as follows:

1. Create a sense of urgency (Chapter 3 - Leading Change).
2. Build a guiding coalition (Chapter 7 - Leadership Activism).
3. Form a strategic vision and initiatives (Chapter 3 - Leading Change).
4. Enlist a volunteer army (Chapter 11 - Mosquito Leadership).
5. Enable action by removing barriers (Chapter 15 - Breaking the Mediocrity Barrier).
6. Generate short-term wins (Chapter 5 - Building the Transformation Model).
7. ustain acceleration (Chapter 12 - Coaching Leadership).
8. Institutionalise the change (Chapter 14 - Creating the Lean Enterprise).

It is not my intention to try to explain Kotter's model in this book, as I wouldn't for one moment pretend to be as qualified as Dr Kotter to do so. However, what I have done is demonstrated where these steps are critical in ensuring that your Lean Transformation, and your role as a Lean Leader, are successful.

Kotter has enhanced his model over time and in his e-book *8 Steps to Accelerate Change in 2015*[9] he observed that:

> **The rate at which our world is changing is increasing,**
> **but our ability to keep up with it is not.**

In the e-Book he speaks about some of the key challenges for organisations, where *Leading with Lean* aims to support you in eradicating:

1. Disengaged employees: disengaged from their roles, colleagues, managers and customers
2. False urgency: consumed by constant activity and firefighting
3. Complacency: lulled into thinking that what got us here will get us there
4. Lopsided organisations: focussed more on management than on leadership
5. Siloed: known more for boundaries than gateways

As you help to take your organisation through the Lean Transformation, they will experience the change curve as the above elements are challenged and the status quo becomes the enemy of excellence change leadership is therefore a large part of the Lean Leader's portfolio of competencies.

TYPO

You can't please all of the people all of the time

One of my most important learning points of change was when I was visiting Omron[10] during a Kaikaku (see Chapter 10) visit in 2008. There, they talked about the 2:6:2 rule of change management, whereby for every 10 people in your organisation you will have two enthusiasts who are advocates of the change, six passive members who are ready to move in the direction of least resistance, and two active detractors of the change who will be vocal in their disagreement of what is happening and can potentially disrupt the process and take the passive group in the wrong direction for the organisation's transformation.

The advice that our group received was that we often spend too much time on the detractors, expending a lot of time and effort in an attempt to convince them that they should come along with the change. However, the time spent with this cohort is time that you are not spending with the other 80% and the most effective use of our time is to work with the advocates for change to bring along the passive team members.

We must, of course, be careful not to completely ignore the detractors but some form of isolation as a result of their non-involvement in the successes that we create with the majority can, and in my experience will, bring some of them along. Nevertheless, be prepared for the fact that, for some, the direction of the change will not suit them and they will need to move onto pastures new. In this case, wish them well and accept that you can't please all of the people all of the time. Along with the leadership Team, you must establish the strategy for managing the few exits that you will have, especially where it might be a person with a strong influence, through position, character or simply length of service.

[handwritten margin note: GET THE "WRONG" PEOPLE OFF THE BUS]

I am not intending to give the impression that a Lean Transformation will result in an increased attrition rate, as in fact it is normally quite the opposite. However, change creates uncertainty and no matter how well your communication and change leadership is run, some people will be disaffected and will ultimately leave. Any attempt that you make to keep everyone on board, regardless of their resistance, will result in an overload and ineffective change leadership and will stall, or significantly delay, the transformation.

As the lone violinist you must accept that not everyone will stop to enjoy the new theme tune of the organisation, regardless of the efforts that you put into change leadership. Your advocates for change will be your most potent allies but the trick is to convert them from advocates to activists, which I will discuss later in the book. When you gain their activist engagement, they will bring the passive employees rapidly along.

" THE PERSON WHO KNOWS THE MOST ABOUT DIGGING DITCHES IS THE ONE HOLDING THE SHOVEL"

Engaging employees

TYPO

Earlier in this chapter I mentioned the importance of engaging employees, our colleagues, in the 'Why?' of the organisation. Change leadership is ultimately about getting the vast majority of the organisation to embrace the vision and to make it happen through a significant change in behaviour and, ultimately, the culture of the organisation. The Lean Leader is fortunate in the respect that Lean Thinking, unlike the vast majority of transformational approaches, requires that the people who do the work and not a group of 'business improvement experts' of some form, are the ones to change the way that it is done. There is an absolute need for Lean experts and I will cover this aspect later in the book. However, the Lean experts are not going to make the change in the ways of working but will rather help to enable the team members with the thinking and tools to change it themselves. It may be a clichéd metaphor by now but this really is the difference between 'giving a man a fish' and 'teaching him to fish'.

NOT THE 'MBB's

SHORT CUTS DON'T LAST

However, there is an unfortunate challenge to be overcome in this regard, as it takes longer (in the short term) to do it this way than it does to simply get in there and make the change. Nevertheless, it is the only way to sustain and maintain the results and to then be able to build on them through continuous improvement. For most organisations there is no way that they could possibly recruit sufficient numbers of Lean experts to do the improvement work, nor could they or afford to have them on the payroll. This is both impractical and ineffective when compared with the Lean Thinking approach, which is to have the people doing the work trained, certified and practising as Lean Practitioners and, through continued practice, becoming Lean experts.

BUILD INTERNAL RESOURCES

The Lean Transformation approach will therefore need to have this engagement built into it through the development of its people by training, coaching and certification as Lean Practitioners. This competency will be built 'at the Gemba', as they implement daily Kaizen and participate in Kaizen events on a regular basis.

In the Lean Transformation of the Philips Consumer Lifestyle Manufacturing Sites, through the deployment of the approach outlined above, employee engagement scores, measured independently by an external provider, were raised from levels of around 50-60% to over 80% and in most cases above to what was considered the high-performance norm.

Engaging the leadership

As mentioned above, one of the issues that the Lean Leader will face is the slower relative progress that they will make with the Lean Thinking approach in comparison to

? PRODUCT FAMILY MATRIX ?

an expert-led project approach. Getting results through our people, instead of for them through expert improvement resources, takes more time and we therefore need to utilise one of the guidelines of Kotter's model and focus on some 'quick wins'.

One of the best ways to do this is to take a model value stream approach, whereby we focus on a value stream, or part thereof, which is complicated enough, and of sufficient scale, to demonstrate that Lean Thinking works in our organisation but is of sufficient complexity and size that it enables us to achieve significant results in a reasonable time frame. What we are looking for is to be able to demonstrate to our leadership within around three months that something big is happening and, within around six to nine months, have proven it beyond doubt.

Linking this back to the Why, the model value stream must address the case for change and the vision of where we need to get to and must deliver against the metrics that we have established, such as improving time to market, gross margin, quality, cost, delivery performance, or whatever really matters to the business and will compel our leadership to become engaged in this transformation. Whilst you have been deploying the model line, the 2:6:2 rule will most likely have been a reality in your Leadership and this will be a watershed moment for the transformation.

This isn't working in isolation from the engagement of the general population of employees, as the model value stream approach is designed to engage both the people involved in the model value stream but also those not involved, as they see the improvements for their colleagues and start to wonder when they can also become involved. It is at this point that we're starting to move our deployment from push to pull.

NOT THE WHOLE ELEPHANT, BUT A DECENTLY BIG CHUNK
- 3 MONTHS PROGRESS
- 6-9 " MOMENTUM

HANSEI

Before moving onto the next chapter, please take a few moments to reflect.
When it comes to your own way of working, what are:

1. Your key learning points?

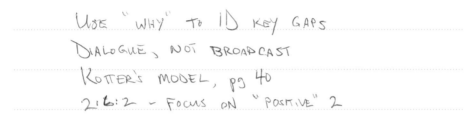

USE "WHY" TO ID KEY GAPS
DIALOGUE, NOT BROADCAST
KOTTER'S MODEL, pg 40
2:6:2 - FOCUS ON "POSITIVE" 2

2. The changes that you could make?

- LEARN HOW TO TAKE & RESPOND TO INPUTS FROM THE WHOLE

? - ALTERNATIVES TO PRODUCT FAMILY MATRIX TO ID MODEL VALUE STREAM?

3. Current problems that they would help to solve?

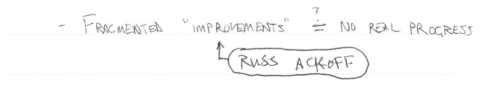

- FRAGMENTED "IMPROVEMENTS" = NO REAL PROGRESS
  RUSS ACKOFF

4. BUILDING CAPABILITY

The importance of conscious incompetence

Knowing what you don't know is an extremely important part of learning and is an essential trait of the Lean Leader. This enlightened humility is the best antidote to an effect, identified by Dunning and Kruger,[1] whereby the inexperienced who are unable to identify their own incompetence have inflated self-assessments of their competence.

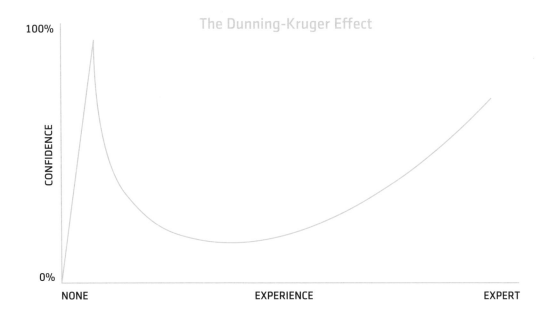

The Dunning-Kruger effect

This is a trait that cannot be tolerated in a Lean Leader, as this will translate as arrogance to colleagues and will be a major barrier to learning. The Lean Leader therefore needs to ensure that they learn how to identify their own competence blind spots and therefore be able to help others.

This transition toward continuous learning, both as an individual and an organisation, follows four main steps:

1. **Unconscious Incompetence:** At its best this can be described as blissful ignorance and in rare cases is a great enabler of innovation, as it allows people to attain results that normal paradigms may prevent them from achieving. However, generally this is not the case and not knowing what you don't know is a real disabler of advancement. The most effective way to tackle this is to ensure that the required competencies and levels are known and that we measure our competence level to expose the gaps based on fact. This requires a willingness and acceptance of competency gaps being an opportunity to drive performance and not an implicit weakness.

2. **Conscious Incompetence:** Once we have realised what we don't know, we can start to learn and this is an exciting time, particularly during periods of transformation. In this phase we can read, experiment, study, hire external resources, team up with colleagues and other organisations to build solutions and fill knowledge gaps. Again, by being fact-based and measuring our improvement, we can ensure that we manage the learning and our effectiveness.

3. **Conscious Competence:** This is the part of the cycle where we get good at doing whatever it is that we've been learning to do and will even start to create new insights and knowledge in this area. Here we start to create experts in the subject. Where there are multiple people going through this learning, we can harness the 'fast learners' to bring others along through training and coaching and, through learning systems, can share the learning to accelerate our organisational knowledge.

4. **Unconscious Competence:** At this stage we do things without even thinking and know things that we're not even conscious of knowing. This is true mastery but only when we are also able to shift back into conscious competence to teach and coach others when necessary. In fact, that is one of the key criteria of measuring a subject-matter expert but not all are able to make the switch back into conscious competence, whilst for the Lean master, this is absolutely essential.

" LEARNING STARTS WITH WHAT THE LEARNER KNOWS

ONE OF THESE IS A TYPO

The Competency Learning Cycle is, for the most part, followed unconsciously and it is critical in a high-performing organisation that we manage these phases and assist our team members to navigate the learning cycle as a core part of our organisation's development into a learning organisation and to become successful in our Lean Transformation.

INCOMPETENCE   COMPETENCE

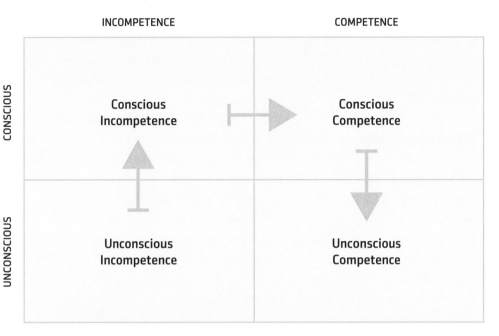

The conscious-competence learning matrix

Developing the right Lean expertise

The skill of being able to realise conscious incompetence and, when skilled, to drop back
into conscious competence to train and coach others is not natural to all people and
only a few are able to do this really well. I'm sure that you must know, or have known,
people who were almost geniuses at what they do, be it in their field of work, hobby
or sport, but find it impossible to explain exactly how they do it or to teach you how to
move through the learning cycle.

3 ANDELL GUYS

This relates directly to the task of employing people with the 'Lean DNA' to drive Lean
Transformations and is a challenge that I've had to undertake and have observed a num-
ber of times. The usual shortcut is to employ people who obviously do have the Lean
DNA, having many years of experience in one of the world-class Lean organisations.
However, a caution here is that not all will know how to build or create the environment
and the organisational capability to make it happen.

They can tell you what is missing and why you need it but not how to build it and, in
my experience, the creator-builder is a rare breed; probably no more than 5% of those
people who even have the experience in one of the role-model organisations.

There are, unfortunately, no shortcuts to employing the right people for this task and in
my experience it is therefore incumbent upon an organisation to have developed the

COROLLARY: NO INDIVIDUAL HUMAN DOES, OR EVEN CAN, KNOW IT ALL.

NEXT CHAPTERS SHOULD HELP WITH DEVELOPING THE PLAN...

strategy for their Lean Transformation, with a clear vision of where they want to get to, described in hard and soft KPIs (key performance indicators), and a plan of how to get there. From this plan, capability and competency gaps can be identified and a combination of consultancy support, external hires and internal development can be used to close those gaps.

Hiring consultants

Once you have determined where your gaps are, hiring consultancy support is a great way to i) quickly fill the gaps in terms of numbers and competency and ii) bring in external experience and benchmarking. However, it is a particularly challenging task, with a common pitfall being that the organisation relinquishes its ownership of the Transformation to the consultants under the misguided aim of increasing the speed of transformation.

On the contrary, it must be a prerequisite of any engagement with a consultancy firm that 3 fundamental principles are in place:

CONSULTANTS DON'T "RUN" THE TRANSFORMATION, THEY SUPPORT IT.

1. The consultants are there to support and develop the organisation's staff and must not engage or run any activities without a member of the organisation in the lead;
2. All training materials and intellectual property used or created during the transformation are the property of the client;
3. Knowledge transfer is one of the KPIs for the measurement of the success of the engagement and must be measured as objectively as possible, for example by number of certified practitioners and the amount of transformation-model training materials and standard work in place.

All of the staff to be used by the consultancy firm must be approved by the organisation to ensure that they have sufficient expertise and have the soft skills to manage the transformation. It must be clear by now that the Lean Leader's hands-on involvement is a necessity and that the hiring of consultants is not an easy option but, in some ways, more challenging than internally resourcing.

However, the use of some form of consultancy support, both at the onset and at particular times during the transformation, is in most cases the only way to bring in sufficiently skilled resources in a reasonable time-frame and to build the Lean Transformation approach with sufficient external expertise.

The consultancy support is therefore the starting point of capability building and not an alternative to the external hires or the internal development routes.

External hires

By definition, as you are not yet a world-class Lean Enterprise, you are unlikely to have a critical mass of Lean experts in your organisation and therefore, just as with hiring consultants, buying in Lean experts from outside is a great way of bringing in the expertise that you will need, except that, unlike with the hiring of consultants, the aim is to recruit long-term employees who will make a great contribution as Lean Leaders. Nevertheless, as I discussed earlier in this Chapter, simply hiring someone with the right 'badge' on their CV in terms of having worked at one of the Lean role model companies is not a guarantee, as we must ensure that they know how to create the environment for Lean Thinking and not simply what it should look like and how to work in it when it exists. This isn't easy and due diligence in employing people with the right ability to collaborate in visualising what the future should look like, identifying the current state, creating the Transformation Plan and driving its execution is crucial. Again, using consultants can support this by firstly relieving pressure to hire quickly and secondly supporting the recruitment process.

The recruitment process for the external hires can be used as a model for the organisation's future approach, as it should ensure that the process, while requiring up-front investment, increases the effectiveness and retention of the people who are employed by the organisation. There is some great advice on the recruitment process by Christine Lagorio-Chafkin of Inc.,[2] providing input for each step:

1. **Job Description:** This should describe the future that you want for the Lean expert, the way that you expect them to act and the elements of the role that are most critical to delivering the Lean Transformation and to providing a clear job title. Critical to the job description is to not only focus on the best parts of the role but to also be honest about the potential 'deal breakers' for potential candidates, for example if travel is likely to be 50% of the role, ensure that this is clear in the job description. This will be the template for the job advertisement but in the latter ensure that any in-company jargon is either translated into plain language or explained fully, but ideally jargon should be non-existent.

2. **Be Competitive:** The role must be positioned in the organisation at the right grading and pay scale, so sufficient time should be spent with the human resources partner to ensure that this is done based upon the organisation's policies and benchmarking in the market. A caveat here is not to overpay for people. While we want to hire great people, who will be Lean Leaders in our organisation, this should be possible without remunerating them at a level that will alienate their colleagues. Remember to highlight any non-salary benefits that you have, such as healthcare, pension, childcare benefits or flexible working practices. Also ensure that the high level of influence that the position provides and career prospects are highlighted.

COMPETE FOR BEST, DON'T ALIENATE PEERS

3. **Find better candidates:** A truism in recruitment is that if the best candidates don't know about the job, they won't apply, and so ensuring that you have the right route to the best candidates is critical. Consider using specialised recruitment agencies, particularly where your organisation is inexperienced in this field or doesn't have the capacity in its HR department, but their use should be screened to ensure that they truly know this marketplace and will add value. Whilst their commissions can be off-putting, the business case can be compelling when we compare the impact of hiring the right candidate versus hiring no candidate or, even worse, the wrong candidate. As you hire the right candidates, don't overlook using their networks. In the era of LinkedIn, premium membership can allow you access to the same pool of candidates that was previously the domain of professional recruiters.

4. **Shortlist well:** Determining who to shortlist, of the many applications that you will hopefully receive, is a challenge in itself but, as with most things allied to Lean Thinking, it will be easier if you are well prepared. In this case a well written job description will allow us to assess the CVs of the applicants against the key criteria. Therefore, for a Lean master posting, we would be able to assess the applicants on, for example, their tenure in roles of the right seniority, experience in comparable scale organisations, multisite transformations, functional fit (e.g. manufacturing, sales, R&D), coaching experience and other elements that we consider key. From this we will be able to shortlist and undertake interviews with those that we deem most appropriate for the role.

5. **Interview better:** The interview process has to be more than a simple face-to-face discussion. Instead it should be a thorough dialogue with candidates who will be interviewing us as much as we are them. This should progress with a strong sense of urgency and quite quickly but this should not be confused with rushing, as thorough preparation will make it a fast but effective process. A typical sequence that I use is as follows:

   a. Telephone Interview of around half an hour to confirm the shortlisting and validate any ambiguity;
   b. In-person interviews with the interview panel;
   c. A Lean Simulation to assess their problem-solving and team-working skills.

Parts b. and c. work best when the candidates are brought in on the same day and the panel meets them on a carousel, allowing a direct comparison without the risk of time-lag influencing the panel members. This approach also allows the Lean Simulation to be run for the candidates as a team, allowing us to assess them in direct comparison with each other.

The panel needs to be balanced and should include the Lean Leader but also members from the businesses or functions that the person will be working for and with, as well as an HR partner. This balance will allow not only technical but also softer skills to be assessed. One caveat around this is to be careful not to hire people who are a fit for the organisation, the reason being that we want to make a significant change in our ways of working and so we need people who will challenge the status quo rather than fit into it. As the motivational speaker, Tony Robbins,[3] once famously said:

If you do what you've always done, you'll get what you've always gotten.

Ultimately, if we want to hire 'change agents' rather than 'same agents', we will need to ensure that the recruitment process is focussed on bringing in people who, to a certain extent, provide a contrast to our current culture.

Internal development

In the next chapter I will outline the importance of the Lean Certification Programme in the transformation model. However, for now it suffices to highlight the value of a certification programme in the development of internal candidates for three main reasons:

[handwritten margin note: SOFT SKILLS CAN BE HARD - TO I.D. - TO BUILD - TO USE]

1. Ensuring a standardised methodology for the training, coaching and certification of our people in Lean Thinking;
2. Embedding Lean Thinking into our employees' daily work by integrating 'learning by doing' and on-the-job coaching into the certification path;
3. Providing an incentive to learn about Lean through a recognised certification that provides a sense of achievement and the opportunity to demonstrate a new skill.

The development of our people will be core to the remit of any external consultancy that we hire and also central to the job description of the external hires. The vision should be that we move from a probable baseline of <1-2% internally certified employees to 100% in the future state. The certification level will be graduated (from Lean foundation through to Lean master) and the 100% level will be at the first level of certification only.

However, even at this first level, our people will understand the fundamentals of Lean Thinking, such as daily management, problem solving and Kaizen, and be able to participate actively in the Lean Transformation.

Through this Internal development of our people, we would expect that over time we would move from filling all Lean expert roles with external hires and consultants in the starting phase, to filling >80% internally after 5 years, that all of our senior leaders will have reached an advanced level of certification and that a large number of them would have rotated through at least one Lean Transformation role.

Distributed expertise

As mentioned in the prior section, whilst all employees will ultimately be certified in Lean Thinking, this will be at the first level of certification, a level that I like to call 'Lean Foundation'. We will further require people at the advanced level of certification, with those being the cohort of people who are supporting people on a daily basis in their daily management, problem solving and Kaizen activities. These will be the line managers throughout the chain and, in line with 'Span of Control', we would expect to have around one person certified at the Lean advanced level for every 10 people in the team.

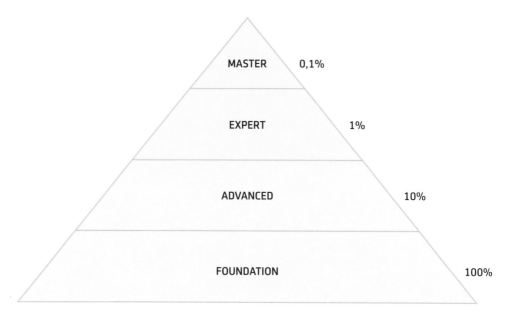

MASTER   0,1%

EXPERT   1%

ADVANCED   10%

FOUNDATION   100%

The levels of Lean Certification

Whilst in the future state we would expect to see our line managers certified at the expert level, in the early days we would expect that this will predominantly be the reserve of our Lean champions and coaches in the functions and businesses, the people who are driving the Lean Transformation on a daily basis. Again, we would expect that the span of control will be around 10 and thus that we would have approximately one Lean expert for every 10 Lean advanced certified personnel, and hence for every 100 employees.
At the highest level of certification are our Lean masters, who are co-creating the vision with the senior leadership, and which will be a relatively small number of people, around one for every 1000 employees. Nevertheless, in a global organisation with, say 100,000 employees, we would still need around 100 Lean masters, which requires a significant combination of recruitment, training and coaching.
I hope this chapter has made it clear that the learning elements of the Lean Transformation, and the demands it places on the Lean Leader, are significant and that an understanding of the Learning Cycle, combined with developing the right Lean expertise are absolute necessities and worthy of a high degree of focus.

HANSEI

Before moving onto the next chapter, please take a few moments to reflect.
When it comes to your own way of working, what are:

1. Your key learning points?

- FIND PEOPLE WHO CAN LEAD, NOT JUST DO
- NOT ALL ABOUT "FIT" — SOME FRESH EYES
- ACCOUNT FOR MORE THAN PROCESS/DATA SKILLS

2. The changes that you could make?

- PLAN FOR WHO GETS WHAT CERTIFICATION, AND WHEN
- ADJUST AS WE SEE WHO TAKES TO IT

3. Current problems that they would help to solve?

- BUREAUCRATIC "SELECTION" OF CANDIDATES

HOW DO WE DEVELOP
- SHOP FLOOR ENVIRONMENT WHERE ALL CONTRIBUTE TO ONGOING IMPROVEMENTS?
- ASSOCIATE SKILLS & COMFORT
- LINE MGT LEADERSHIP

5. BUILDING THE TRANSFORMATION MODEL

[handwritten: IT'S LESS OF A DESTINATION, MORE LIKE 'THE SHOES WE PUT ON EVERY MORNING']

Why we need a transformation model

The transformation of your organisation into a Lean Thinking and Operationally Excellent Enterprise is a long journey and will require the involvement of every single employee and the maintenance of the change programme on an ongoing basis. *[handwritten: PLUS CHEERFUL YET DOGGED PERSISTENCE]*
In Chapter 3 I discussed Kotter's Change Leadership model and the steps that are required to successfully deliver our Lean Transformation and, throughout the Transformation, it is important to ensure that the organisation is sustaining its change enablers, which can be summarised with the initials VCRSP:

1. **Vision:** The Leadership must maintain a consistent vision throughout the change, ensuring that the organisation is focussed on its end-state and has a 'North Star' upon which to focus.

2. **Commitment:** In the first instance the senior leadership must be fully committed to the transformation and, over time, this must permeate the whole organisation.

3. **Resources:** The appropriate level of resources, people and funding must be available to support the transformation and must be maintained at the right level for the duration of the change.

4. **Skills:** While we need sufficient people, they must also have the right skillset to be able to support the transformation. These resources, as covered in the previous chapter, must be hired or developed in a thorough manner.

5. **Plan:** For excellent execution of the transformation, a thoroughly prepared and detailed plan must be created and managed throughout the transformation. *[handwritten: REAL TIME ADJUSTMENTS]*

During the transformation the organisation will move from the initially small scope of establishing the case for change and establishing the pilot through to a state whereby the whole organisation is transforming and the scope is one which cannot possibly be overseen by one person.
For many Lean Transformations, this transition from relatively small-scale to large-scale, whole-organisation deployment is the moment of failure, as the replication and rigour of *[handwritten: LOST]*

[handwritten: ↳ RISK MANAGEMENT ++]

the initial approach is inevitably lost. For some smaller organisations this may not be an issue, as the scale is insufficient to disrupt the deployment. However, for most organisations, particularly multi-location and multi-country ones, it is a common cause of failure. Additionally, in the initial stages of a Lean Transformation, the enthusiasm and high level of management attention will compensate for any gaps in the deployment approach. Nevertheless, this will not be infinite and, after a short time, often when the initial victory of the pilot has been declared, focus will wane and any gaps in the deployment methodology will begin to impact the efficacy of the transformation.

HONEYMOON WITH EXPERTS

To avoid the scalability limitations and management attention loss, along with ensuring that the change leadership approach is built into the deployment, a Lean Transformation Model is required to guide us through our Lean Journey. It is, in effect, the change blueprint for our organisation, keeping us to plan whenever we start to drift off-course, whatever the cause may be, and will ensure that we maintain the VCRSP conditions that are essential to our long-term success. This subject is covered in more detail in Chapter 15.

TYPO

IT'S LESS THE "TOOLS", MORE THE LEADERSHIP

Build it with excellence in mind

You intend to create excellence in your organisation through the deployment of the Lean Transformation Model and it should therefore be designed and built to be excellent. I will provide some guidance on how to build this model but, to populate its content and to learn how to deploy Lean Thinking effectively, you must go to Gemba, finding those Companies that have done it well and learn from them. Toyota is of course the exemplary model but there are also a notable few who have achieved, or are on the road to, excellence, such as Honeywell,[1] Danaher,[2] Virginia Mason,[3] Porsche[4] and Unipart[5] among others.

EXTERNAL — ONE GOOD SIGN IS WHEN SOME GEMBA IS INTERNAL

STRYKER KALAMAZOO, 2005

As I discussed in Chapter 4, you may also wish to engage with a consultancy who can help you to develop both your approach and the people in your organisation who will enable it. However, the consultancy must teach and coach your Lean experts in how to do this, not do it for them, and therefore searching for that true partner who can support the development of your organisation is critical if you don't have sufficient Lean experts in your organisation already.

The Lean Deployment Model that you build must take into account the best knowledge available out there and you should not be reticent in the opportunity to 'proudly steal' those best practices, whilst being inquisitive enough to ensure that you fully understand what your role model companies really did, taking into account that only a few of the people that you speak with will be consciously competent, with the majority not necessarily knowing what they know. You must therefore be careful that you can differentiate

THOUGHT PROCESS, NOT JUST THE CURRENT "SOLUTION"

between a true understanding of what worked and a retrospective rationalisation. The model must manage a certain dichotomy, in that it needs to have a rigidity in its approach that will lead you through with the stamina and consistency that are fundamental to success. However, it must be sufficiently agile to deliver transformation in the different functional and business areas of the organisation and across geographical and cultural boundaries without the Lean Leaders losing their fidelity to the model. This is a challenging paradox but, with a model that focusses on the people development and Lean Thinking requirements while allowing freedom to select the tools, it is possible.

INCLUDING KNOWING WHEN NOT TO USE

The VIRAL model

VIRAL is the acronym that I have used for a best practice approach to Lean Transformation that I have developed. VIRAL covers the 5 stages of deployment that are needed to truly embed Lean Thinking into an organisation:

1. Vision
2. Impact
3. Replication
4. Amplification
5. Legacy

Change leadership is embedded into the approach, which combines the development of people and overall organisational capability in parallel. It is intended to provide a robust and sustainable model for transformation and is similar in thinking to models used by a number of world-class organisations.

Whilst the model isn't rigidly sequential, therefore allowing for the utilisation of tools and techniques from later stages as required by the business, it does require that all elements of a stage are completely fulfilled before the organisation can be 'released' from that stage. This establishes a maturity measurement and avoids the model being used in a 'pick-'n-mix' manner. Nevertheless, finishing a stage must never be a business target in itself; instead it should simply be the outcome of doing the right things for the business. Therefore, we plan to exit each stage in a particular timeframe but, where this doesn't occur, we problem solve as to why, rather than 'project managing' an exit.

LIKELY A TOUGH HABIT TO BREAK, BUT VITAL

The model can operate at multiple levels in an organisation, dependent upon its size. For example, in a single-site organisation, it would be used at just one level, as the whole business can be managed within the single framework. However, at the scale of a global organisation we would have multiple levels, as the deployment model would need to be executed for the overall organisation, at the next level for each of the core processes of idea-to-market, market-to-order and order-to-cash and also for each of the enabling functions, such as IT, HR, finance, and so on. Within each of these areas, there would be a third level of deployment, at the individual location, such as a manufacturing site, innovation site or a sales organisation in a market.

Stage 1: Vision

In this first stage, the readiness of the organisation for change is established and the leadership are trained in the basics of Lean Thinking. This is when the Leadership Team brings together the key stakeholders to establish the case for change, as described in Chapter 3, and the communication plan is established and initiated.

The model value stream will have been selected and agreed, with Hoshin Kanri (Chapter 6), sometimes called policy deployment, introduced to ensure that the execution of the strategy is effective and that the breakthrough activities are planned, resourced and aligned across the business. This is a relatively short stage but is critical to ensuring that everyone is committed to the transformation and the concepts of Lean Thinking and that they all believe that this approach is the one that will best attain their collective vision.

Before Stage 1 is finished, the following would be required:

- The case for change agreed and the future state vision set, with ambitious targets
- Stakeholder analysis and communication plan in place
- Lean Transformation Plan agreed
- Model value stream selected and ambitious targets to improve agreed
- Hoshin Kanri developed and deployment started
- Lean champion for the deployment area recruited
- Leadership for the deployment area trained in the basics of Lean Thinking and the Transformation Model

[handwritten note: HOW IS THIS SIMILAR OR DIFFERENT FROM 'FOUNDATION'?]

Stage 2: Impact

[handwritten note: BUILD CREDIBILITY]

As described in Chapter 3, the establishment of some quick wins is critical to the engagement of all employees but, in particular, the leadership. Trying to deploy Lean Thinking across the whole enterprise, assuming an organisation larger than a few dozen people, is a little like trying to boil an ocean; you'll put a lot of energy into it with very little to show for it. This stage is therefore designed to achieve two objectives:

1. Achieve significant results in a relatively short period of time, with the aim to show a big change within three months and sustainable, significant results in six to nine months. *(handwritten note: GAIN GROUND)*

2. Allow a lot of learning about what works and what doesn't work in a small enough part of the value stream so that we can modify our approach before scaling. *(handwritten note: ADJUST)*

In this stage a model value stream of average complexity and large enough to be meaningful is selected, and Lean Thinking is thoroughly deployed. In essence we want to see this value stream transformed in the context of Womack and Jones' five steps of Lean Thinking:

1. Establish value for the customer.
2. Make the value stream visible.
3. Create flow.
4. So that the customer can pull the value.
5. Strive for Perfection.

This will entail establishing the fundamental Lean elements of daily management, leader standard work, standardised work, problem solving, Kaizen, 5S, value stream mapping and implementing the Lean Toolkit as necessary for the particular value stream. Concurrently, the development of the people in the value stream will be undertaken, creating Lean Practitioners who, at the end of the stage, will be capable of 'striving for perfection'. The model value stream becomes our own vision of excellence and proof that Lean Thinking can be applied with a high, positive, business impact in our organisation just as well as it can in others, making this a great way of silencing those who claim that 'we are not Toyota' or use other similar statements of resistance to change.

To achieve this, one of the first things that we do is to take a few key people, normally the leadership of the area where the model value stream will be, on a Kaikaku experience (Chapter 10), a visit (usually) to external parties who can act as a 'vision of excellence' for the team, enabling them to visualise the type of environment and culture that they can create. This is intended to inspire the team and to provide them with the confidence that the transformation is viable. This visit is not 'industrial tourism' and is managed in such a way as to maximise the learning. The group who attends is obliged to communicate and share their learning to the wider team.

(handwritten note: SEE WHAT = / SEE IT POSSIBLE / SUCCEEDING)

Dependent upon the scale of the organisation, a number of model value streams could be running, with the caveat that the Lean expertise to support them must be in place and that overstretching at this stage risks failure.

One key lesson for the leadership at this stage will be the level of Leadership Activism (Chapter 7) required. I often joke that at the end of Stage 1 the leadership have voted for Christmas but by the end of Stage 2 they have realised that they are the turkeys. Joking aside, this will be a critical time for the deployment as the leadership team and the line managers will come under pressure from the change as they, and the organisation, go through the change curve.[6]

The middle management are under particular pressure as they realise that the type of interventional problem solving they built their career on is no longer necessary and is, in fact, counter-productive to Lean Thinking. The Lean experts need to place particular attention on the coaching of this cohort, as they can move into detractor mode if they are not supported in changing their way of leadership into one of a coach and not a director of people.

At the end of this stage, the Model Value Stream will be testimony to what Lean Thinking can achieve in your organisation. You will no longer need to show colleagues what others have done and instead you will be able to demonstrate that Lean Thinking also works for your enterprise, with colleagues who can testify to that. In fact, it is likely that those colleagues who now work in the model value stream will be the best advertisement for the Lean Transformation and the pull from others to be next will be massive. This creates a great deal of opportunity but also risk, as scaling too quickly can over-stress the programme.

Before leaving Stage 2 behind, the following would be required:

- The Lean Fundamentals are in place and at a mature level.
- The ambitious improvement targets of the model value stream have been achieved.
- All model value stream's team members are certified at the Lean foundation level and the appropriate number at the advanced level (circa. 10%).
- The value stream has been visualised in its current state and the future state vision defined.
- The initial future state has been achieved and the next iteration is planned.

Whilst the aim is to have significant results in six to nine months, it is common for the maturity of the Lean Fundamentals and certification of people to take a little longer, as the people-based changes typically take longer than the tool-based changes. Nevertheless, by this point you will see such a high degree of motivation that the Lean experts are no longer encouraging people to engage or speed up but are struggling to keep up, as the team members move forward at pace.

↑ FROM "PUSH" TO "PULL"

Stage 3: Replication

In the third stage of the VIRAL model we replicate our learning across the rest of the organisation. This is by far the longest of the stages, as it will essentially entail replicating what has been done in only a few model value streams across multiple areas. It is critical that during Stage 2 we have built sufficient capacity and capability in terms of Lean champions to support the deployment and, if we've done a good enough job of developing our people in the model value stream, some of this will be used in the replication areas.

PEOPLE

Getting the replication plan right is critical and we must adhere to three key rules when doing so:

DON'T DISCOURAGE IMITATORS, BUT DON'T INVEST, YET

1. Prioritise based upon business need, linked to your Hoshin; we have finite resources and must get the biggest impact for our resource investment.
2. Accept that team members in areas not currently under deployment will start to adopt the new ways of working; don't be distracted by this and don't deploy resources there. It's great that they want to do it and by all means let them learn but don't lose focus.
3. We cannot just cut and paste into the next deployment areas. There will be solutions that can be replicated but the new ways of working need to be adopted through the change process just as in the model value streams; it will go quicker than in the model areas but slower than a top-down, expert-led approach. However, it is the only way to ensure sustainability.

PEOPLE NEED TO LEARN THE APPROACH

For a large organisation the replication will take multiple years but the results will start to come through from an early stage. This is where the deployment model really starts to prevent entropy, as it instils discipline and prevents victory from being declared too soon and rigour lost.

It is extremely important to re-emphasise that Lean Thinking is not simply for the manufacturing arena and therefore in this stage the roll-out must cover the whole enterprise from new product development through to sales and after-sales support.

At the end of this stage all personnel, that is 100% of the employees at all levels of the

IMPLIES MORE THAN JUST ATTENDING CLASS

organisation, must be certified as practitioners of Lean at the foundation level [100%]. The advanced level certifications may still be progressing but the structure for certification and the curriculum and plans must be in place and in the process of execution.

Before leaving Stage 3, the following would be required:

- The Lean Fundamentals are in place and at a mature level across all value streams.
- Ambitious improvement targets have been achieved.
- 100% of team members are certified at the Lean foundation level [100%] and the appropriate number at the advanced, expert and master levels are either certified or following their certification plans.
- The value streams have been visualised to current state and the future state visions defined.
- The initial future states have been achieved and the next iterations are planned.

→ "MINIMUM VIABLE PRODUCT"

Stage 4: Amplification

As first the model value stream(s) and later the replication sites come to the end of their Stage 2 and 3 activities, they will be running with an extremely high level of performance that is better than it has ever been. However, if we are to reach true world-class excellence, we need to break through and implement new approaches that change the way that we operate. Essentially, up to now we've ensured that the design intent of our way of working has been met; we're operating with excellence as we had planned to do. However, in the amplification stage we need to change the design intent of our operating model.

It could be, for example, that we had a promised delivery lead time of 10 days, with an OTIF (on time in full) commitment of 98% but had historically been delivering with a high degree of variation and hence an OTIF of <85%. In Stages 2 and 3 we've solved that and are now consistently delivering to the 10-day commitment at 99.9% OTIF. However, in the amplification stage not only have we decided to meet our commitment to the customer but we've understood from them that an improvement to two days would make us their preferred supplier and drive sales. This becomes one of the breakthrough targets of our amplification stage.

As mentioned at the beginning of this chapter, it is not the intent that the model is rigidly sequential, so Stage 4 activities can legitimately be worked on while a value stream is still in Stage 2 or 3. However, the model will hold the site to that stage until it can prove that it has embedded the foundations of excellence so that the Stage 4 activities can be built upon, avoiding their subsequent collapse. This also ensures that the amplification activities are not undertaken using the wrong type of thinking, as, in the example of lead-time, by increasing inventory instead of reducing value stream lead-time.

To support this, Lean accounting practices[7] must be implemented to prevent standard cost accounting techniques causing conflict between the Lean Team and the accountants, due to waste reduction leading to lower inventories or lower OEEs (overall equipment effectiveness) as a result of stopping production when there is no customer demand.

At the end of this stage, all Lean experts will be fully certified and Lean Thinking will be practised at every level of the organisation. By this point, the Lean Certifications of your organisation should be recognised externally by other organisations and your people a sought-after resource for others. However, because of the opportunities within your organisation for these people, your attrition rate is still lower than it was before the start of the transformation and those that do leave are ambassadors and unpaid recruiters for your organisation.

Before Stage 4 can be left behind, the following would be required:

- Breakthrough improvements have been made in the value streams.
- The Lean Maturity of the organisation is such that it is simply the way that people work.
- 100% of team members are certified at the Lean foundation level and the appropriate number are fully certified at the advanced, expert and master levels.
- The future state vision value stream maps have been achieved and the next iteration designed.
- Lean accounting practices ensure that business decisions are made using Lean thinking rather than a sub-optimal focus.

Stage 5: Legacy

In the final stage no new approaches, tools or techniques are implemented but rather the sustainability of the deployment is confirmed. At the end of Stage 4 each area of the business has truly been able to claim excellence in the way that they operate and at this moment a number of your locations will have been recognised by external bodies. For example, the Philips Shaver Factory in the Netherlands and the Philips Avent Baby

(UNLESS DELIBERATELY DISMANTLED)

Products Factory in the UK have both won industry leading awards in the past two years as a direct result of their Lean Transformations.[8]

However, it is critical that we give the model time to fully mature, so in this final stage we are going to reinforce the systems in the business to ensure that we can confidently release it from deployment with the knowledge that Hoshin-led breakthrough, continuous improvement and daily management are simply the modus operandi of the organisation.

The Lean masters and champions' roles have changed by Stage 5, as Lean Thinking is part of the DNA of the organisation and the people who do the work are perfectly capable of the daily management activities, problem solving and Kaizen. Instead, the Lean resources reduce in number as some of them rotate into new operational roles, whilst those remaining start to work on more strategic activities, supporting business expansions, new product introductions, mergers and acquisitions and setting up centres of excellence.

By this point our whole organisation is staffed by Lean experts and simply put, we have ensured that the Lean Transformation has left a Legacy of Excellence in the organisation that will persist ad infinitum.

Before leaving Stage 5, the following would be required:

- The vision of excellence has been renewed.
- The results achieved in the previous four stages have been sustained and continuous improvement and a Kaizen culture are delivering above-average performance improvement.
- Continuous improvement is institutionalised, with a living Kaizen culture.
- The competence of employees is such that support is no longer required for daily management, problem solving and Kaizen activities.

The management of the deployment

It must be obvious by now that the management of a Lean Transformation isn't easy. While the Model will help to maintain consistency across the deployment, it also takes a lot of effort to educate the Lean experts, manage the programme and maintain support in this long-term approach. However, what I have not yet covered are the metrics for performance, which are the key element for maintaining the support of the leadership. There are two elements to these:

1. **Business Results:** These must be directly linked to the business' Hoshin and made specific (e.g. sales, EBITA, inventory, time to market, etc.) for each part of the value stream. Additionally, people metrics, such as employee engagement, retention, safety, Kaizen, and competency will be included.

2. **Lean Maturity:** The behavioural and tool application elements of Lean will be measured through a maturity matrix, using a 'proof point' assessment of the area being assessed. This is usually a five-point scale, from low to high maturity per element, calibrated between the value stream leadership team and a Lean expert. Examples of these elements are items such as the policy deployment approach, training and coaching, load levelling and the problem solving approach. The intention of this is to ensure not only that the business results are achieved, but that this is done in a sustainable way.

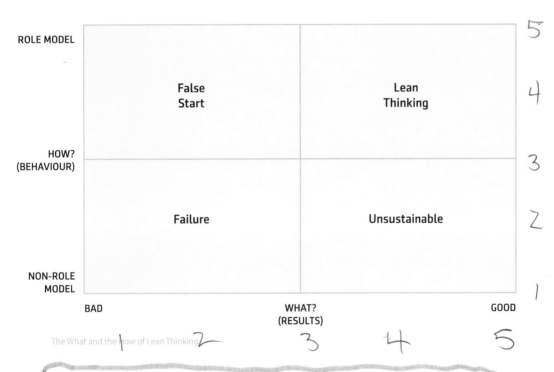

The What and the How of Lean Thinking

Managing the deployment is a tough job, having to hold and maintain a belief in the vision of excellence many years down the road, whilst ensuring that the short-term wins that will maintain oxygen in the transformation are achieved. The lone violinist metaphor comes back at this point, as the Lean Leader will need to maintain fidelity to the Transformation Model, despite the many challenges driven by anxiety and a desire for faster results.

However, just as in the metaphor, the Lean Leader cannot simply play their tune and hope that people stop to listen; they must maintain the communication, the connections with the sponsors of the programme and ensure that there is an audience for their music. Sometimes they will have to let some battles go, keeping their eye on the overall war on waste in the organisation, accepting that some parts of the enterprise will move more slowly than others.

Being the Lean Leader is not easy but then that's why world class is only for the few.

HANSEI

Before moving onto the next chapter, please take a few moments to reflect.
When it comes to your own way of working, what are:

1. Your key learning points?

- LEADERSHIP > TOOLS
- MINDSET > "FIXES"
- VIRAL MODEL / SIGNS OF "GRADUATION" FROM PHASES

2. The changes that you could make?

- FOCUS ON VISION > PROCESS OPPORTUNITIES (TO START)
- PLAN FOR BREAKTHROUGH LEAPS, BEYOND FIXING ISSUES
  - SEEK "UNHEARD OF" OUTCOMES

3. Current problems that they would help to solve?

- "ONE AND DONE" APPROACH
- BACK SLIDING

PART II
LEARNING TO LEAD

"TIMWOOD" CAPTURES PROCESS WASTE

THERE ALSO EXIST FORMS OF ORGANIZATIONAL WASTE -

- "OVERBURDEN OF INITIATIVES"
- IGNORING VALID CONCERNS
- DISREGARDING SKILL SETS & STAKEHOLDERS
- POORLY MANAGED MEETINGS
- NEEDLESS MEETINGS
- WORKING ON N.V.A. INITIATIVES
- DOG & PONY SHOWS (INCLUDING PREP)
- STRATEGY SESSIONS WITH NO FOLLOW THROUGH

6. HOSHIN KANRI

[handwritten note: "ONE FORM OR ANOTHER" LEAVES A LOT OF LEEWAY TO PAY LIP SERVICE WITHOUT TRULY "DOING" MUCH OF ANYTHING]

The need for Hoshin Kanri

Hoshin Kanri, or policy deployment, is an approach known by most people and quite a few organisations use it in one form or another. However, despite this the statistics in terms of the need for a more effective execution of strategy are clear:[1]

- Less than 15% of companies routinely track how they perform over how they thought that they were going to perform.
- 95% of employees don't understand their company's strategy.
- Less than 27% of employees have access to their company's strategic plan.
- 86% of executive teams spend less than one hour a month reviewing strategy.
- 90% of companies fail to execute their strategies successfully.

[handwritten note: OPPORTUNITY TO DEPICT AS AN INTER-RELATIONSHIP DIAGRAPH]

There are a few large organisations for whom Hoshin Kanri is a clear and integral part of how they consistently deliver breakthrough performance in the execution of their strategy. However, I have also seen a number of smaller organisations prospering with this approach, and the clarity that it brings for the team members is great to see. Most importantly, it significantly reduces overburdening and feeling of a lack of direction among many employees and deals with the root cause of a significant part of the waste that we find in an organisation; the overburden of initiatives.

Eric Abrahamson, in his book *Change without Pain*[2], describes the significant impact of initiative overload on organisations and their people, looking at the vast number of academic studies in the field, including over 5000 on employee overwork and burnout. His central argument is that firms can achieve superior long-term and short-term performance by reducing the amount of highly disruptive change. My belief is that Hoshin Kanri is the way in which this can be strategically managed.

The leadership problem

Given that less than 15% of companies track performance against plan, meaning that over 85% of companies will not realise how badly they are executing their strategies, it is hardly surprising that 90% of companies fail to execute their strategies successfully. Furthermore, as around 86% of executive teams spend less than one hour a month reviewing strategy, they would appear to be more involved in the day-to-day problems of the *handwritten note at top: NOT JUST A "ONE-AND-DONE"*

handwritten note in left margin (vertical): CAN'T SOLVE "ALL" THE PROBLEMS WITHOUT INVOLVING "ALL" THE PEOPLE → LEAN FOUNDATION

business than they are in steering the future direction. Given this, it is hardly surprising that the leaders of most organisations don't take the time to implement a methodology that would ensure excellence in the execution of their strategy.

It should therefore be clear that, if we are to successfully transform our business using a Lean approach, the Lean Leader must ensure that Hoshin Kanri is embedded into the leadership's way of working. It shouldn't be a surprise by now that this will include not only implementing the tool but also establishing a commitment from the leadership to rebalance their time allocation away from daily firefighting toward strategy execution. Fortunately, the deployment of Lean Thinking will enable our people to solve problems in a structured way and will reduce the expectation that leaders should solve all of the problems.

For the Lean Leader this will be another moment to engage the leadership in the music that they are playing, demonstrating the beauty of the new approach and the benefits that it will bring to them, their people and the business.

handwritten note at right: MY ANALOGY — TOO BUSY SHOVELING, TO GAS UP THE BULLDOZER

Too busy to improve

The secret ingredient of business success

Hoshin Kanri is what I call the secret ingredient of business success, as it is found in some form or another in all of the most successful businesses, probably most famously at Danaher for the way in which they have used it to grow their business at an average of around 20% year on year for over 20 years.

It is a structured methodology for the translation of strategy into execution and Hoshin Kanri, like many of the Lean Management methodologies, is a Japanese term, which simply translated means 'direction needle' and 'control logic'. Hoshin Kanri is therefore a methodology for the logical management of the execution of the organisation's strategic direction.

Hoshin Kanri follows the PDCA cycle in its approach with an annual rhythm and typically a three-to-five-year time horizon. In the planning phase, the major differences between Hoshin Kanri and a typical approach to the deployment of strategy are two-fold:

1. Decisions are actively made on what to do but, most importantly, which of the many opportunities the organisation will NOT take up. Companies that adopt Hoshin Kanri accept that having too many priorities is the equivalent of having no priorities. Some opportunities will have to be sacrificed, not because they are not good initiatives but because the organisation simply doesn't have the resources to pursue them. Other things are more important and focus is required to do them well.

2. The answer to how the strategy will be delivered is delegated to the appropriate level of the organisation through a process called 'catch-ball', meaning that those people who will need to deliver are also empowered to determine the best way to deliver. They also get to provide input on Item 1, to ensure that the decision made on the priorities is the correct one.

As you may have gleaned from this, the planning phase typically takes longer than it would in a traditional approach and is very thorough and inclusive, with the strategy creation and targets initially set at the top level of the organisation but a great deal of the "how to achieve' determined at the most appropriate level of the organisation through an iterative approach. However, what this thorough planning allows is a rigorous discipline of execution once the organisation moves into the do, check and act phases of the cycle.

It is typical that this planning will take place during the third and fourth quarters of the organisation's financial year to ensure that the plans are ready for execution on day one of the new financial year. What is important to note here is that this is an ongoing cycle rather than distinct planning per year and therefore the annual plan is simply the continuation of the longer-term strategic plan.

The plans are, of course, linked to the annual budget or AOP (annual operating plan) of the organisation and it should be clear how the initiatives that are chosen will contribute to the business performance improvements, of which there will be two contributing components:

1. Hoshin Kanri initiatives and
2. Continuous improvement / Kaizen.

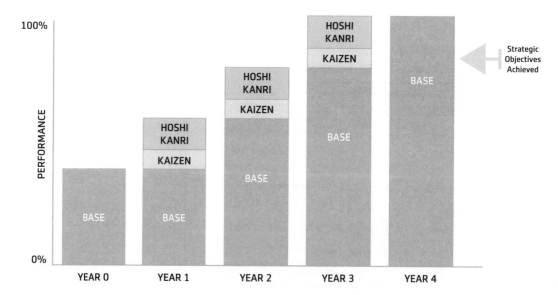

Annual performance improvement through a combination of Hoshin and Kaizen improvement

Throughout the annual cycle, the daily execution of the plans will be managed by the owner and their execution team, whilst the next level leadership team will review on a regular basis, typically monthly. Depending on the number of levels in the organisation, these reviews will roll up to the top of the organisation. However, the level of detail will decline as the reviews move upward.

This PDCA cycle runs continuously and ensures that there is support for the initiative teams where it is required and that execution is effective. Where changes in the business environment occur, changes to priorities can be made but only within the Hoshin

Kanri review structure, to ensure that changes are made for good reasons only and not because of a whim or fancy. The important thing about the process is that it recognises that there will always be more good ideas than resources and therefore the prioritisation and focus on choices is paramount to a successful execution.

The X-Matrix

As the Hoshin Kanri approach is rolled out across the organisation, it is important that a standardised approach is used to deploy the methodology, as it will cascade from the top level of leadership through the different levels of the business and so a standard approach is essential to ensuring that it is the content that is discussed and not the format.

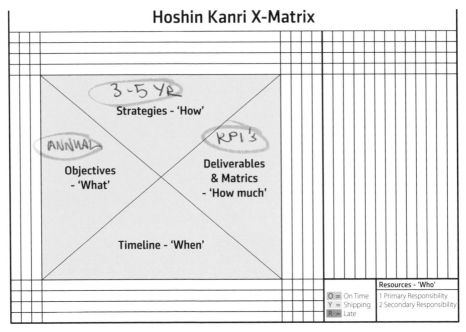

The Hoshin Kanri X-matrix

Whilst there are a number of formats available, one of the most popular is the X-Matrix, which brings with it a certain elegance in terms of its readability. The beauty of the format is that the strategic objectives for the next three to five years, the annual objectives for the current planning year, the initiatives to deliver the annual objectives and the KPIs that will be improved by the initiatives may be viewed on one piece of paper, or one PowerPoint slide.

Behind this will be an A3[3] problem solving document for each of the initiatives, detailing the problem statement, target condition, root causes and the countermeasures to reach the target condition. From this A3, the implementation plan is made and can be used to allocate the tasks to the different parts of the organisation and ensure that the resources are in place.

The X-Matrix facilitates the cascading of initiatives from the top level of the organisation to the subsequent levels, whereby an initiative will become an annual objective for the next level, which will then have sub-initiatives that are appropriate for its level. Dependent upon the size of the organisation, the cascade could go for three to four levels.

To give an example of this, assume that one of the strategic objectives of a company was to grow its revenue by 50% over the next five years while maintaining its EBITA. This annual objective for the financial year might be to increase revenue by 15%, which might translate into one initiative related to expanding sales into the North American market. This initiative could then be cascaded into the North American sales organisation, who would make this one of their annual objectives. They would decide how to do this through the catch-ball process explained earlier, ensuring that they had sufficient resources and capabilities in place to do this and completing the A3 and implementation plan.

This was one simple example but it obviously becomes much more complex as we look at the multiple initiatives that are normally prevalent in an organisation. Nevertheless, this is another of the advantages of the X-Matrix as it makes this problem visible quite quickly and facilitates the tough discussions and difficult decisions necessary to focus on only those initiatives which will truly deliver our strategic objectives with the resources and capabilities that we have. Where we don't have sufficient resources or capability to achieve them, this will also be exposed and decisions can be made about either scaling back ambitions or putting in place a realistic plan to increase our capacity to deliver on them.

→ DON'T MAKE PROMISES WE CAN'T KEEP

Ritual planning

WALK THE TALK

As discussed earlier in the chapter, leaders must invest sufficiently in the development and execution of strategy if it is to be successful. They must plan the allocation of their time to do this and ensure rigour and discipline in adherence. The best way to do this is through a technique called leader standard work[4] (LSW), one of the fundamentals of Lean Thinking. A significant part of this is simply planning your time accordingly and a previous manager of mine coined the term 'ritual planning' to describe the essence of what this is.

ENDORPHINES →

One of the biggest challenges for a manager, and something that the Lean Leader must support, is to let go of the daily firefighting that they will inevitably be involved in. This is difficult to give up on as it is addictive and, despite what many managers will tell you, I observe a willing participation by most, which in my opinion is due to the feeling of achievement that it gives in the short term.

Managers must be weaned off the firefighting 'drug' and the 'intravenous email' that enables if the Lean Leader is to achieve the focus that is needed to make Hoshin Kanri, and hence strategy execution, work. The Lean Leader therefore needs to invest signifi-cant time in teaching and coaching the leadership in setting up their 'ritual planning' and ultimately their Leader Standard Work.

Given that around 86% of executive leadership teams spend less than one hour per month on reviewing their strategy and that the ideal is more like 107 hours,[5] which is around 70% of their time, the gap between current state and future state is usually mas-sive. Even at the mid-managerial level we would expect around 60 hours per month of their time to be dedicated to breakthrough activity and it would thus be disingenuous of me to suggest that you ought to ask your leadership to make such an immediate leap. Realistically, the other elements of the Lean Transformation, enabling daily management, problem solving and a Kaizen culture to permeate the work floor, are required before the leadership can fully eradicate their indulgence in firefighting, so we need to start with a realistic commitment.

→ START HERE

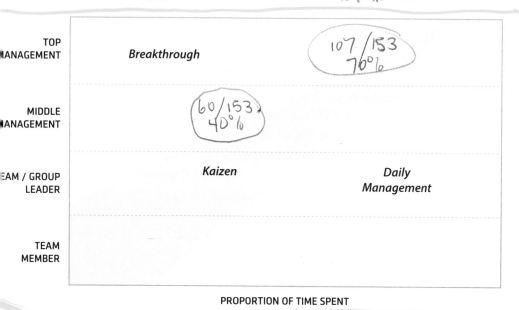

TOP MANAGEMENT	*Breakthrough*	107/153 76%	
MIDDLE MANAGEMENT	60/153 40%		
TEAM / GROUP LEADER		*Kaizen*	*Daily Management*
TEAM MEMBER			

PROPORTION OF TIME SPENT

Time allocation guidelines for the different levels of an organisation

An approach that I've used effectively is to agree with the leadership team to initially commit to allocating their weekly time in the following ratios:

- Daily management - 50% or 20 hours per week
- Strategy / Hoshin Kanri - 20% or 8 hours per week
- People development - 10% or 4 hours per week
- Flex time - 20% or 8 hours per week

This time is then planned in their calendar, with as much coordination of the daily management and strategy time as possible to ensure that collaboration is possible amongst team members. The people development time is the structured time that they will spend on one-to-one performance and development reviews with their team members, remembering that people development and coaching is an on-going exercise and should also happen informally during all other activities.

Flextime is an important element of this planning. Just as we would not plan to run a machine 100% of the time, we should not plan our people's calendars to tie up 100% of their time. We therefore need to provide them with some overflow time in case of additional problem-solving time requirements from one of the other three categories or simply for some 'Hansei time' to reflect upon things and make decisions in a positive manner.

What this means in terms of a 'day in the life of' the leader is that they will spend time 'at the Gemba' to undertake daily management for around four hours per day, attending CommCell (communication cell) meetings, supporting problem solving and being involved in Kaizen activity. They will also likely have one or two half-hour development meetings with their people and spend around one to two hours working on strategy / Hoshin activities. In their flex time of one to two hours, they will catch up on any of the problem solving that came out of the earlier elements.

By helping the leadership to work in a more structured manner, focussing on increasing their time spent on the breakthrough activities, the Lean Leader will take a great stride toward effective Hoshin Kanri, embedding Lean Thinking into the organisation and creating an enabler of the other elements of the Lean Transformation.

[handwritten note: MORE CLARITY: WHICH OF THESE ACTIVITIES RESIDES UNDER WHICH TIME ALLOCATION CATEGORY]

HANSEI

Before moving onto the next chapter, please take a few moments to reflect.
When it comes to your own way of working, what are:

1. Your key learning points?

ORG'L WASTE — INCLUDING WORK ON "WRONG" THINGS

TIME ON FIREFIGHTING ↓

START W/ KAIZEN ON SHOP FLOOR

2. The changes that you could make?

BONE UP ON HOSHIN KANRI

RITUAL PLANNING

3. Current problems that they would help to solve?

STRENGTHEN LEAN LEADER SKILLS

IMPROVE PERSONAL TIME MANAGEMENT

7. LEADERSHIP ACTIVISM

Being a lean pig

Question: In a bacon and egg breakfast,
what's the difference between the chicken and the pig?
Answer: The chicken is involved, but the pig is committed!

Whilst this metaphor only stretches so far, what it represents is that we need leaders truly committed to making the change to a culture where excellence is expected, who not only 'talk the talk' but also 'walk the walk'.

So what does this mean for the Lean Leader? Well, put simply, they must be the pig, not the chicken and they must create as many pigs as possible in their organisation for the Lean Transformation to succeed. Those Lean-Thinking organisations that are world-class are only that successful because a critical mass in the company became lean pigs.

Whilst I accept that we shouldn't go around telling people that they need to become pigs -- that is just for the purposes of the metaphor -- it is essential that our Lean Transformation includes a way of transitioning the people in our organisation to the new way of thinking in a committed manner.

This involves some serious training, coaching and engagement to get there. In my experience, this is the only way to get to the level of commitment required. However, this is the difference between having advocates for change and activists for change, which is far more than nuance or semantics but is a tangible difference in the way that the leader will operate and model Lean Thinking.

Let me give an example which I have witnessed a number of times. A certain area of the business has embarked upon the deployment of Lean and appears to have the necessary enablers in place. There is a Lean champion, training has been set up, and the leadership team supports the other teams in making the time to set up their daily management processes, including CommCell Boards, standardised work and so on, as well as value stream mapping to identify their future state vision and a Kaizen event plan to deliver it. However, when it comes to the daily management, value stream mapping and Kaizen events, the leaders are nowhere to be seen. They do not practise Leader Standard Work and continue to manage through emails and 'shoot-from-the-hip' problem solving. Despite articulating their support for the Lean Programme, they fail to demonstrate a real commitment through active involvement in the change, the Leadership Activism that we require if we are to be successful. In this example, the Lean Deployment is doomed to mediocrity and will fail to be transformational. Some improvements to the business will occur, as the people on the ground will use what they've been taught to make improvements to their ways of working but the destination of operational excellence will not be reached.

The Lean Leader is a coach amongst their colleagues, continuously encouraging and teaching them how to become activists. This will require humility and a willingness to make mistakes and show 'conscious incompetence' in front of their teams. However, once the initial fear is overcome, what they will observe is an increased respect and appreciation from their teams as they see them embodying the change that they want, modelling the new ways of working and experimenting with them. This is an important moment in the transformation.

Being more than an advocate

Discovering an Activist Leader is a special moment and I have been fortunate to work with and meet a few. Within the company that I currently work, Royal Philips, I have worked with and coached a number of our executives who have been responsible for the deployment of Lean in their area of responsibility. Many of them have demonstrated Activist Leadership, always being prepared to be actively involved in the deployment of Lean Thinking and having invested the time for training and certification at the Lean advanced level. In these cases, the Lean Transformation has prospered and their team members have maintained a high motivation for the deployment.

I have also researched a number of Lean Transformations to understand the role that the Activist Leader plays in its success. Three leaders who really impressed me are Art Byrne (who amongst other things transformed Wiremold and wrote a motivating book about it entitled *The Lean Turnaround*)[1], Professor John J Oliver OBE (former CEO of Leyland Trucks who turned around the business with what he termed 'radical employee engagement')[2] and Dr Gary Kaplin, MD (who as CEO of Virginia Mason, a Healthcare Provider in WA, USA, has led his company to become one of the most successful Lean Transformation successes in the healthcare industry and to a leading position in North American healthcare provision).[3]

Dr Kaplin is an inspiring Lean Leader, who, along with the Virginia Mason board, took a transparent and humble approach to addressing their case for change at the beginning of the 21st century:

- Survival (losing money for the first time in their history)
- Poor retention of the best people

- Loss of organisational vision
- Leadership change
- A defective product

The concept of the defective product is an interesting approach to viewing healthcare and is an eye opener in terms of what it means for patients, as it refers to a historical 3-4% defect rate. This means that for every 100 patient encounters there were three to four defects, which could be anything from no record of an appointment all the way through to an avoidable death.

As Dr Kaplin stated in his address of the St Luke's Health System Summit in 2013:

> *...if the aviation industry had this sort of defect rate, planes would fall out of the sky every day; if flat-screen TVs had these kinds of defect rates we wouldn't buy them...*

The story started in the year 2000 when the Virginia Mason board asked Dr Kaplin and his leadership team the simple question:

Who is your customer?

Their response was predictable:

The patient.

However, the board retorted that if that was the case, things wouldn't be the way that they were:

- Processes were designed around medical professionals and staff, not patients
- Hundreds of millions of dollars are spent in the healthcare industry for waiting rooms, 'places for patients to hurry up, be on time and wait for us' as Kaplin described them
- If everything is alright with their test results, patients are sent home by Friday afternoon, if not, they wait through the weekend until Monday

By facing the reality of the situation they tackled some of the paradigms prevalent in the Healthcare industry and one of the most courageous things done by Dr Kaplin and the board was to go public about a preventable death that had a major impact on their

Lean Transformation. Despite already being three years into the deployment of Lean, they refocussed to a single organisational goal for the years 2004 through to 2006, of protecting patients from avoidable harm.

A reassuring element of the approach that the team at Virginia Mason have taken is that they have not tried to reinvent Lean for their industry, although they have been creative with their approach, even calling their Lean System the Virginia Mason Production System (VMPS). This is a mature approach and would appear to be a critical factor of the mindset required to be successful in a Lean Transformation. In this case it was driven by their Activist Leader.

Another element of Activist Leadership is the way that Dr Kaplin has driven Virginia Mason to undertake detailed value stream mapping of their current states (finding that typically >90% of the time fails to add value) to enable the significant improvements that they've made in their performance. They have also taken a granular approach. However, Dr Kaplin is clear about the role of the Lean Leader:

> *As leaders there are technical changes, Lean, there's the toolbox, it's the improvement method ... but you need a critical mass to feel urgency, you need to have visible and committed leadership; not advocacy leadership; I was a great advocate leader ... my job was to get all the resources from our department and keep administration off of our backs ... but that's not what we need now...*

As a result of the 15+ years of Lean Transformation, Virginia Mason has made a fantastic leap forward in performance and care for patients. In 2010 they were awarded Top Hospital of the Decade by the Leapfrog Group and have since featured regularly in the Top 100 Hospitals in America list.[4]

The cultural change in their organisation is tangible and is led from the top, with another great quote from Kaplin demonstrating this:

> *... we've got a $2.7 trillion industry, we've got enough money in healthcare ... We need to change our mindset from scarcity to one of abundance. It's what we do with our resources that counts.*

Virginia Mason and Dr Kaplin have demonstrated that, with true Lean Leadership and a Lean Transformation linked to the business strategy, an organisation can fundamentally transform its performance.

Creating Activist Leaders

[handwritten note: LEADERSHIP IS BEHAVIOR, NOT "RANK"]

Leading with Lean requires our leaders to be activists like Dr Kaplin but it doesn't mean that we only need the activism of the CEO, the C-Suite and the senior leadership. Rather, we need all leaders, from CEO to team leader on the shop-floor, to be Activist Leaders and we must create the environment that will support and enable this.

This means that the Lean Leader must create scale in the proliferation of the coaching of our leaders at every level. This is where the VIRAL model plays a big part, as it ensures that we build the Lean Leadership across the organisation through the training, coaching and certification of our leaders.

At the shop-floor level we train our team leaders, group leaders and area managers in leading the change through workshop-based training and certification to the lean advanced level. At the senior level we train with high-intensity Lean Leadership classes to simulate the change leadership that they are required to make for themselves and lead others through, leading to their own certification at the lean advanced level.

[handwritten note: "LEAN ADVANCED" HAS CUSTOM PATHWAYS BASED ON ROLES]

Whilst we're doing this, we're also developing the Lean champions and Lean masters who will scale this across the organisation. This is another reason why we use the model value stream approach, developing a critical mass of advocate leaders before we scale up. As discussed in Chapter 4, we distribute the expertise throughout the organisation with our 'rule of ten' Lean Certification ratio of 1:10:100:1000 (master: expert: advanced: foundation).

In Chapter 3 I also talked about the 2:6:2 rule of engagement, whereby on average in every group of 10 people there will be two advocates. While we ultimately want activists, not advocates, these are still the best people to build into activists and so should be our initial target group as we begin the transformation. For example, in Stages 1 and 2 of the VIRAL model we identify and recruit these people and, as they begin to grow as activists, we should see the passive team members starting to take note and move into the advocacy and ultimately activist camp.

As this builds, we reach the point at which we will have the critical mass that we need to scale the Lean Transformation across the whole enterprise and will find ourselves in the best form of Lean Transformation, a people-focussed Lean Transformation.

[handwritten note: CRITICAL MASS (TN?) OF LEADERS — ROSTERS OF EXPERTISE → • OVERLAP BUT NOT THE SAME • LEADERSHIP CAN OCCUR AT ANY LEVEL OF LEAN EXPERTISE]

HANSEI

Before moving onto the next chapter, please take a few moments to reflect.
When it comes to your own way of working, what are:

1. Your key learning points?

- CUSTOMIZE PATHWAYS TO CERTIFICATION (ESP. ADVANCED), BASED ON ROLES IN THE ORGN
- TOP MGT MUST LIVE THEIR DAILY LIVES AS ROLE MODELS

2. The changes that you could make?

- SEEK TO MODEL "DAILY LIFE" BEHAVIOR

3. Current problems that they would help to solve?

- BETTER FOCUS ON THE IMPORTANT
- STRONGER CASE TO "SELL" LEAN

8. DISCIPLINE AS A COMPETITIVE ADVANTAGE

The simplicity of discipline

Jim Rohn[1] once said that:

Discipline is the bridge between goals and accomplishment.

I think that this statement has a certain elegance in explaining the simplicity that discipline can bring. We all want to accomplish our goals, but it is a truism that those who reach them are the ones who have been prepared to put in the effort needed, which requires discipline.

To illustrate this point, last year I wrote an article about a problem-solving review that reminded me of the childhood nursery rhyme about the old woman who swallowed the fly. In the article I reminded the reader that, whilst we still don't know why she swallowed that fly, we do know that it created a chain of events leading to the ingestion of a horse, which according to the nursery rhyme was less than conducive to her good health.

The reason that I was prompted to use this metaphor was that the problem-solving process that I was reviewing had made the common mistake of not getting to the root cause and instead taking countermeasures against the symptoms. The result was that the team had accepted that a workaround to the correct process, caused by a lack of discipline in the original process, was a legitimate process in its own right. They had therefore tried to find the root cause of the failure of that process. The resulting countermeasures increased the complexity of a process that should not have existed in the first place, if only the root cause of the lack of adherence to the standard process had been addressed.

[handwritten margin note: THEY TRIED R.C.A. ON A WORK AROUND]

Despite my best efforts, I could not prevent the explanation in the paragraph above from being complicated, so you can imagine what the actual process looked like and how challenging it must have been to work with while ensuring quality. This was, once again, a great proof point of the simplicity that discipline brings and the complexity created by not having the will to ensure that discipline.

737 MAX ??

Another elegant statement, for which I do not know the author, is:

Discipline is just choosing between what you want now and what you want the most.

The reason that I like this statement is that I feel that it articulates well why we struggle with discipline so much in organisations, particularly in larger ones where people are perhaps detached from the consequence of a lack of discipline. Either it will not fall to them to resolve or it will take so long to become a consequence that it is not a concern to them at the time when they have to make the decision.

What generally happens is that the person making the decision on which action to take will often know what the correct action is in terms of the standard process. This was the case in the example above, in which the decision to ignore the required approach at the beginning of the process was because it was easier (in the short term) not to follow it. For the people making the decision there were little to no consequences and, even where there could have been, they were literally weeks, if not months, away. The effort to follow the process to the standard, and to problem solve where there were issues with the standard, was therefore more than the majority of the people were willing to invest.

"HARDER TO DO IT RIGHT"

The fact of the matter in most organisations is that discipline to processes and standards is often seen as negative, both in terms of stifling the creativity of the individual and in restricting the flexibility of an organisation. However, time after time I see evidence that those organisations which pride themselves on their flexibility within their processes are often simply covering the cracks of failure in earlier steps of the process and expend a lot of time, energy and resources in doing so. Furthermore, the flexibility that they are so proud of is not benefiting the customer but is instead assisting colleagues who have been let down as a result of a process failing due to lack of discipline. The result is that the organisation is not flexible, nor do the individuals have any time to be creative. Most significantly, the customer does not benefit one iota from this so-called flexibility. Additionally, as in the earlier example, additional processes and sub-processes are often created to work around the correct processes, with unofficial SOPs (standard operating procedures), creation of work instructions and different parts of the organisation working in their own ways, which seem to make sense to them. The worst part is that these are very often processes that are rework loops and add no value to the customer and, to compound this, process improvement initiatives 'automate' the process with IT or robotic solutions to make it more efficient.

However, as Drucker[2] once so poignantly said:

EXCEPTION: SOME ORG'NS DON'T DO A GOOD JOB DEVELOPING PROPER STANDARDS

COMPLEXITY = HIDDEN FACTORY

There is nothing so useless as doing efficiently that which should not be done at all.

Just like the old woman who tried to solve the problem of the swallowed fly through the addition of other animals further up the food chain, many organisations spend a considerable amount of time adding processes without adding value in an attempt to solve the problems in their existing processes.

By getting to the true root causes of the issues, putting in place countermeasures and applying discipline around the execution of the process standards, the organisation can deliver high performance, better flexibility due to shorter lead times and free up the time of its employees to be creative. The reality is that lack of discipline creates significant complexity, whereas discipline provides simplicity in an organisation, something which most greatly need.

Discipline as an advantage

As mentioned earlier, focussing on discipline is often seen in a negative light, a way of controlling people and limiting both personality and creativity. However, in my view the critical factor is whether the focus is on driving discipline in processes or in applying discipline to people. For example, consider the ineffectiveness of a large proportion of meetings, where it is not uncommon for people to arrive late and unprepared, and for a significant proportion of the meeting to be unproductive, making it ineffective overall. If we try to solve this problem with increased discipline for our people, we are unlikely to make any long-term improvement, as we will encounter both passive and active resistance when we tell people how to behave. However, if we take countermeasures to the root causes of underperformance, focussing on reducing the inhibitors and increasing the promoters of effective meetings, we take a process approach to engendering discipline and will engage our people in improving the meeting process. This may be a nuanced difference, but in reality it will result in the creation of a standardised, effective meeting culture in the organisation, driven by the people who make it work.

As retired Lieutenant General Frank Kearney[3] said:

Disciplined processes create agile organisations.

The most agile organisations are those which have a high degree of discipline, which essentially means that they have standardised what they already know how to do well and then stuck to it. This has allowed them to spend their time focussing on solving the problems (taking the opportunities) that they don't yet know how to solve.

In his book *Focus*, Daniel Goleman[4] describes how repeatedly practising something, with discipline, allows the brain to move it from the top part, requiring focus and high cognitive energy, to the bottom part, allowing instinctive operation at low cognitive energy. This is essentially unconscious competence and can be achieved in an organisation when we standardise our processes, align them with the current best way of performing the task and then ensure that we have effectively trained everyone who will be working with them.

When we do this, we free up people's cognitive energy to be spent on other things, those activities that will grow the business and improve customer service and operational performance.

Athletes and sports players are a great example of this. Goleman's book gives the example of those great quarterbacks (American football) who are credited with being able to 'see the field'. What they are actually able to do is the result of their thousands of hours of practice, which repays them with an ability to use the low cognitive energy part of their brain. This is true in all areas of life where we want to perform at the top end of the spectrum, be it American football, golf, marketing, public speaking, painting or ballet. Whatever we want to be good at, we must standardise and then have the discipline to continuously practise that standard.

Bringing this back to business, it is therefore essential that we set up our processes in a standardised way and act with the discipline required. Only when we do this will we allow ourselves the time to adequately focus on making the breakthroughs in performance necessary to be the best at what we do. The challenge is that most of us spend our time in perpetual firefighting and some organisations actually promote people on their competence as a firefighter, therefore reinforcing this culture within the organisation. Ironically, working in a culture where firefighting activity is the norm will mean that our people will become highly skilled at it and will become conditioned to it as the standard way of working.

What we therefore need to do is break the habit of firefighting and start to celebrate and recognise those people who use disciplined, standardised approaches to problem solving and upholding process rigour to prevent problems recurring and free up the time to improve the business. To paraphrase Albert Einstein:

Managers firefight problems; leaders prevent them

To do this requires us all to behave differently and for the leadership to take up the challenge to drive the transformation that is required in the business. This takes individual and organisational stamina and a change leadership approach that is consistent and long-term in its thinking. However, what is most important is the mindset that we develop toward operational excellence.

We would never expect to see an athlete or a musician performing at the top of their chosen profession without thousands of hours of practice over many years, so why do we expect to take shortcuts in developing our businesses to be world-class without putting in the disciplined practice that it takes?

We somehow seem to expect that there are formulaic approaches that can be applied and bought in to shortcut the years of practice required to become excellent in the areas that the business needs to be excellent in. This doesn't mean that we cannot learn from others and transform faster than others have done before, but it does mean that we cannot abbreviate the process to the extent that most businesses attempt to do and we must invest the time to consistently execute on the transformation plan.

At this point I think that it's important to clarify that this standardised and disciplined approach to business processes does not mean that we won't improve them or that we don't make step changes when necessary. We must also create a culture of continuous improvement (Kaizen culture) that delivers multiple small, everyday improvements leading to large improvements over time. Combining this with policy deployment (Hoshin Kanri), we will make the step-change improvements that are required where continuous improvement won't suffice.

Once again, we can use the sports world as a metaphor, with the example of Tiger Woods. When he had reached the limits of success that he could master with his 'tried and tested' golf swing, he controversially decided to transform it. He effectively moved his golf swing out of the bottom part of his brain up to the top part and reprogrammed it. Slowly but surely, through hours of practice, his new swing moved into the bottom part. This was a step-change improvement that continuous improvement couldn't have brought him.

We therefore must realise in business that transformation takes time and thus set the right balance between continuous improvement and step-change activity, realising that, in both cases, the ability of the organisation to maintain discipline over the long term is going to make the difference between success and failure. This is where discipline becomes a competitive advantage.

I see dead people!

In the movie *The Sixth Sense*, starring Bruce Willis, the twist of the story is that the child that he is talking to can actually see ghosts and that Willis' character, Dr Malcolm Crowe, is one of those unfortunate souls. This is a surprise to Dr Crowe and not something that he is happy to discover, bringing the sudden realisation that his 'life' will never be the same again.

While it is certainly not as significant as discovering that they are ghosts, when a Lean Leader learns to identify the multitude of waste that exists within an organisation's value streams due to lack of discipline, it is nevertheless a life-changing event, as the more that they learn to see the waste and lack of discipline that is tolerated, the more difficult it is for them to moderate those observations.

At a certain point, everywhere they go and every process that they see contains activity that simply does not add value for the customer but is accepted as 'the way that we do things here'. The challenge for the Lean Leader becomes the coaching of colleagues to see the waste themselves, rather than delivering the (often unwelcome) bad news to them.

This is where the Lean Leader must be smart and ensure that they do not gain a reputation as someone who is negative or unrealistic, even naïve about the way that things need to be done. Instead they should coach problem solving, asking the right questions, to ensure that the waste, and the lack of discipline inherent in its cause, is identified by those who do the work themselves.

Obviously not all waste is caused by lack of adherence to a standard, but I have come to believe very strongly that before we set off down the route of re-engineering or reinventing our processes, we must in the first instance ensure that we're running to standard and observe the performance running as the process was designed. When we do this we often discover that quite a number of the problems that we are encountering are caused by simply not adhering to the current standard and that reinforcement of this, with the requisite training and communication to reinstate it, will provide a significant uplift in performance.

This SDCA (standardise, do, check, act) before PDCA (plan, do, check, act) approach is actually the basis for continuous improvement but is often overlooked and is an excellent way in which the Lean Leader can help to demonstrate to the organisation the value of disciplined execution to standard, followed by problem solving, ultimately leading to Kaizen where necessary.

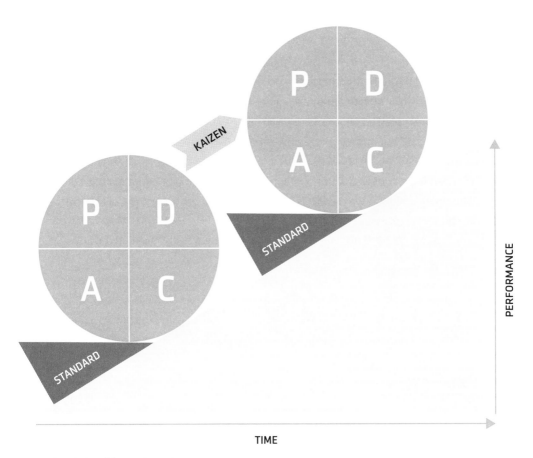

PERFORMANCE

TIME

Standards enabling continuous improvement

Leading discipline

The Lean Leader has a significant task in most organisations if they are to support the move toward disciplined execution. However, this chapter has hopefully demonstrated the value that can be derived through a focus on developing your organisation's disciplined adherence to processes, not by focussing directly on the discipline of the people but on the adherence to the processes. As mentioned earlier, this might sound like nuance but, as with most things in life, nuance can be the difference between collaboration and conflict and so it is important that this subtlety is embraced.

Think about the number of Kaizen events and projects that could be circumvented if running to standard solved the majority of the problems in a particular process. This doesn't mean that you will ignore that process, as we will still want to continuously improve but we can deprioritise it and focus on those processes that truly don't run well when we run them to the standard. This is when we can make fact-based decisions on our priorities.

Think of it like being in an extremely cold house during the winter and realising that heat is being lost through the doors and windows, which are not secured. The processes that are not currently running to standard can be thought of as the doors and windows, which have simply been left open and need to be closed, whilst the processes that are running to standard but don't work are broken panes, which need to be repaired. Somewhere in between, there will be doors and windows that have insufficient insulation and need to be improved. In this metaphor I'm sure that the prioritisation of tasks would be pretty straightforward and it is important that we get to this level of clarity with our business processes.

HANSEI

Before moving onto the next chapter, please take a few moments to reflect. When it comes to your own way of working, what are:

1. Your key learning points?

....

....

....

....

2. The changes that you could make?

....

....

....

....

3. Current problems that they would help to solve?

....

....

....

....

9. VISIBLE LEADERSHIP

Genchi Genbutsu

Genchi Genbutsu is the Japanese term for 'go see' and is critical for the Lean Leader's success. By going to see, Visible Leadership can be achieved and this goes hand in hand with Leadership Activism, going to the Gemba, the place where the work is done, and helping to solve problems. However, the Gemba shouldn't be taken to refer exclusively to a manufacturing shop floor; it can be a workstation in a design office, a call centre, or an operating theatre. It is, in fact, anywhere where the value (and also the waste) is created for the customer. Taiichi Ohno, considered the father of TPS (the Toyota Production System), said it best:

> *Toyota Managers must be sufficiently engaged on the factory floor that they have to wash their hands at least three times a day.*

Being a Visible Leader is one of the critical elements of Lean Thinking and so, if you leave the 'Lean Stuff' to your Lean People, problem solving to 'the experts' and Kaizen events are something that you leave to subordinates, then you will also leave Lean firmly on the side-lines as just another initiative and a tool-based approach.

By going to the Gemba and helping to solve the problem where it is happening; by leading Kaizen events, undertaking Kamishibai and being seen as a Visible Leader; you will begin to live the following Lean Principles:

- Principle 5: Build a culture which stops and fixes problems to get quality right the first time.
- Principle 7: Use visual controls so that no problems are hidden.
- Principle 9: Grow leaders who thoroughly understand the work, live the philosophy and teach it to others.
- Principle 10: Develop exceptional people and teams who follow your company's philosophy.
- Principle 12: Go and see for yourself to thoroughly understand the situation (Genchi Genbutsu).

Being a Visible Leader is not just about being seen but about being seen to support team members in adding value for the customer. By asking the right questions, helping them to solve problems and removing barriers, the Lean Leader will help them to help their customers and will graduate as a 'Leader as a Teacher'. To do this they must help them to make their workplace, and the processes and value streams within it, visual. In virtual environments, such as most creative and transactional environments, this is even more important and the use of tools such as a CommCell (communication cell), visual planning boards and Kanban development boards[1] can be a great way of achieving this visualisation.

An example of a CommCell in a healthcare environment

To quote the wisdom of Ohno once again:

> *Make your workplace into a showcase that can be understood*
> *by everyone at a glance.*

Creating the showcase

Leading with Lean requires that the workplace becomes a showcase of excellence, whereby the status can be understood by everyone at any time and in an interval that is meaningful. This means that the status, say four weeks ago, is not acceptable; it is the status now that matters or, dependent upon the area of the organisation, within a reasonable time interval. This means that on a factory floor the status within the last few seconds or minutes will be visible and in a development environment, within the last few hours or day.

The Lean Leader will encounter some initial scepticism and resistance as they begin their visits to the Gemba, as the employees will suspect that it is the typical visit for show, without real meaning, resulting in potential criticism and additional workload or even a change in priorities and direction. However, the Lean Leader must have the patience to demonstrate, through their activism, that the visits will be often and that they will be meaningful. This will build trust with their team members, resulting in improved engagement and an increased focus on excellence and quality in everything that they do.

To create the showcase, there are three core elements in the system that need to be created:

1. Hoshin Kanri
2. Daily management
3. Problem solving

Hoshin Kanri is so important that I dedicated a chapter to it (Chapter 6). It is, as with most elements of Lean Thinking, very easy to understand as a tool but quite difficult to embed as an element of the culture of the organisation. Nevertheless, its establishment from the top of the organisation is essential and, through the 'catch-ball' method, once objective cascading has been established, their visualisation will ensure that everyone in the organisation sees their contribution to the breakthrough objectives.

When this transparent visualisation of the objective cascade is observed in an organisation it has great impact, as employees can easily select one of the objectives in the area that they are in and speak to the team members about its status. This transparency engenders an inherent openness in the conversation and there is a certain confidence in the demeanour of the people talking about their goals. The Philips AVENT manufacturing site in Glemsford, UK, is a fantastic example of this, whereby everyone in the organisation can show, very clearly, their Hoshin objectives and describe in simple terms their contribution to the business goals.

Daily management is an essential process in a Lean Organisation and relies heavily on making the workplace a showcase. Essentially it is about short interval control, which simply put means that we know as early as possible when there is a problem. An oft-used analogy is that of the captain of a ship, who is navigating to an island.

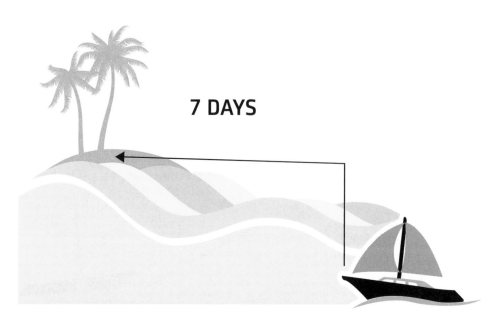

The voyage should take four days. However, in the first iteration of the voyage, she checks her location after four days, finding that the ship has gone off course and that she needs to readjust its navigation. The journey takes seven days to complete.

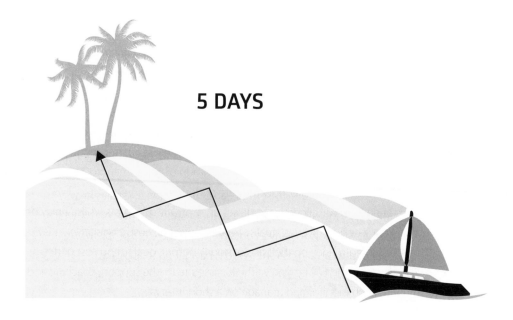

On the second voyage, the Captain adjusts her interval to daily, still having to adjust her course but on a more frequent basis and reducing the voyage duration to only five days.

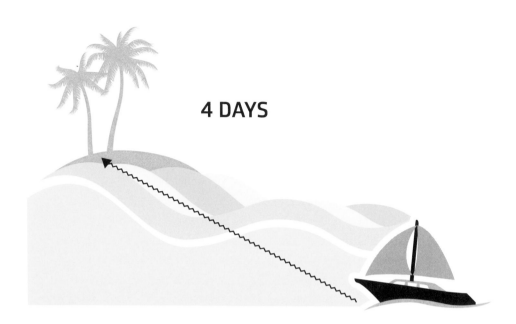

4 DAYS

However, on the third voyage, she makes a check on her navigation on an hourly basis and ensures that the course is almost perfect, delivering 'operational excellence' and a voyage time of only four days.

Whilst the analogy is fictitious, it illustrates the importance of short-interval control and is applicable whether the management is of an FMCG (fast-moving consumer goods) manufacturing line, that of a Boeing 747 or a new-product introduction process. Whatever the process may be, the appropriate short-interval control, visualised to allow a quick understanding and diagnosis of the current performance, is essential.

When implementing short-interval control to support daily management, each area of the organisation will need to think carefully about its leading indicators. Too often enterprises have lagging indicators that tell us how we performed last quarter, month or week and it is one of the biggest challenges of any team, group or department to determine which metrics will tell them, quickly, how they are performing.

Most manufacturing lines will allow this to be set up relatively quickly, as whilst it may be the norm to look at weekly deliveries, quality performance and cost, it is relatively easy to start managing performance on the basis of hourly output, quality and cost performance. The main challenge will be to give the localised team the support, coaching and empowerment to both monitor and manage on a short interval.

Although it may be easier to implement short-interval control in manufacturing, it is just as important to do so in all other areas of the organisation and types of business. What is considered to be a short interval might change, but the reality is that, whether it be a manufacturing line or a new product introduction programme, most organisations wait too long before realising that they are off course.

Whilst short-interval control might be an extremely important part of daily management, it is not its entirety and to ensure that the organisation creates the showcase, it must establish an effective way to visualise, discuss and problem solve performance. This is where the CommCell, or Communication Cell, is a central component of Daily Management, offering a 'performance cockpit' for the team members. Done well, the team members should be able to clearly see and understand their performance, identifying where they have deviations and problem solving to get back on target.

Once again the CommCell at the level of a Lean Tool is simple and easy to set up but the challenge comes in the team and its leader having the right behaviour and competence to utilise it to its full effect. This requires that the team is trained effectively and that a standardised approach is taken to its set-up but at the same time ownership is established in the team. At Royal Philips this has been established through what are called 'Daily Management Boot Camps' where Lean experts take the local leadership and their teams through the establishment of a CommCell based upon a standard, but, through the boot camp, gain its adoption and localisation by the team.

Once the team has a CommCell in place, visualising the people, performance and continuous improvement aspects of their area, they will observe underperformance, or problems. This brings us to the third element of creating the showcase, which is problem solving.

Problem solving

The problem with problem solving is that everyone, in their own way, solves problems. What makes the difference is the method that they use to problem solve. Whilst this book is not intended to delve deep into the Lean Toolkit, problem solving deserves more than just a cursory discussion.

Most teaching of Lean will stress the importance of true root-cause analysis and problem solving at the level of root cause, but this is too simplistic, as another problem with problem solving is that there are too many of them to do them all justice and to truly solve them at root cause. It is for this very reason that most organisations do such a bad job of problem solving, as they begin the process many times but rarely finish due to a lack of time and resources.

It is therefore crucial that in our visual showcase, being the visible leader, we teach prioritisation and the management of problems at the different levels of the organisation. This essentially means that we are going to have certain expectations, the first regarding the number of problems solved at each level of the organisation.

One of the biggest changes that the Lean Leader will establish in an organisation is that the propensity for all problems to be solved at the leadership level will cease. Instead, we will expect over 85% (by number, not scale) of problems to be solved at the Gemba by the teams doing the work. They will identify, prioritise and solve most of the organisation's problems quickly and practically, as we will have provided them with the skills, motivation and empowerment to do so.

Of the less than 15% of problems that escalate above the team leader at the Gemba, around two thirds of them will be solved at the next level, that of the group leader or area manager, meaning that less than 5%, by number, of the remaining problems will get to the senior leadership level. These will, of course, be big problems and require a lot of horsepower to solve but, these are precisely the big problems that are getting in the way of the organisation's ambitions and will become the Hoshin Kanri objectives, the big problems that need to be solved to make performance breakthroughs.

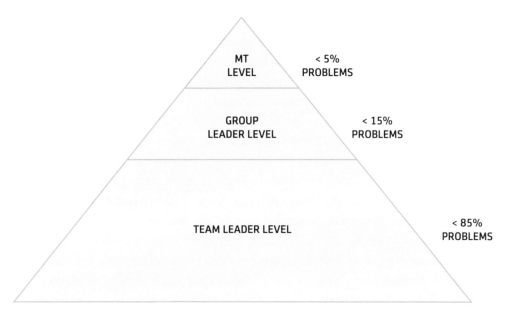

The problem hierarchy

The second expectation is that, at each level, the problems are prioritised. This is best done through a proper definition of the problem, which is also a way of ensuring that the problem to be solved is properly understood and can therefore be satisfactorily solved. There is an old saying that:

A problem properly stated is half solved.

A simple way of establishing the problem statement and one that, with practice, can be done quickly for the smallest of problems, is the 5W + 1H. This approach is sometimes confused with '5 times Why?' (5 X Why?) but should be distinguished from this, as it is earlier in the problem-solving cycle and at this stage, that of defining the problem, we do not actually want to start trying to get to the root cause.

5W + 1H is a very effective problem definition approach for the Lean Leader and is utilised by answering the following six questions:

1. What is the problem?
2. Why is it a problem?
3. Who is it a problem for?
4. When is it a problem?
5. Where is it a problem?
6. How much of a problem is it?

The importance of this approach is that it provides a data-driven approach to defining the problem statement and avoids the team working from personal perception or instinct. The questions have a certain element of overlap and it is not intended to be an exact science but a 'problem statement' should be generated, based upon facts, that adequately answers all of these six questions.

The beauty of this approach is that it both allows the team to determine those problems that may not be that big and provides fact-based evidence to manage stakeholders who may perceive problems to be larger than they really are. Ultimately it should provide the team with a method by which they can rapidly determine which problems they are going to focus on solving, as it is inevitable that they will have more than they can manage in the immediate term.

The team at the Gemba will do this relatively rapidly and will utilise their CommCell, as part of their Daily Management process, to identify problems and then make the decisions on which ones to tackle. An elegant way of doing so is the '3C' of the CommCell, which normally sits under its performance section, and is named to represent the fact that it is made up of columns that read 'Concern', 'Cause' and 'Countermeasure'.

Concern	Cause	Counter-measure	Owner	Due Date	Step
Day sales < target			Phil	22/3	Plan

The 3C document

The team will identify concerns over their performance and rapidly draw up the actual problem statement, determining how big a problem it is. Where it is a low priority, they may decide to take no current action, whereas if it is a moderate problem, they may decide to take some immediate action, although it might be that they don't get to the root cause and instead implement a rapid countermeasure that addresses perhaps the symptoms only and doesn't necessarily address the root cause. However, where the problem is a clear and present issue, they will assign an owner to address it, rapidly.

3C problem solving is great for rapidly prioritising and solving the majority of those >85% of problems that the team will resolve, either on a short-term, symptom-based level, or at the root cause. However, for a few of those problems and especially for those that are escalated to the next level, A3 problem solving will be initiated, where problems are taken by a small team and thoroughly solved, truly addressing the root cause of the problem and implementing countermeasures that will make a difference in the longer term.

In some cases the team at the Gemba may put in place short-term countermeasures to address the symptoms and get better at dealing with the issues that they are dealing with on a daily basis, whilst the overall problem is escalated for the long-term solution that deals with the root cause.

Problem Solving A3: <Headline Problem Title>

RAG Status

Problem definition	Countermeasure development <in order of Root Cause Linkage>
What is the Problem? (Should not include Root Cause or Solution)	
Target setting	
What will Success look like?	Checking results The results will be established through te measurement of:
Root Cause analysis Please see the next slide for the Ishikawa Diagram What are the 2-3 Root Causes to be addressed?	Standardization of succes

Owner:	Date:	Process:

A3 problem solving

Nevertheless, whatever the level that the problem solving is undertaken at, the Lean Leader must ensure that the countermeasures implemented result in a Kaizen, an improvement to the standard, otherwise the countermeasures will be short-term (unsustainable) by nature. This is the part of problem solving that really sets the Lean Organisation apart from traditional organisations.

Kamishibai

The use of Japanese words in Lean Thinking is simultaneously natural, due to its famous Japanese practitioners, and potentially a barrier to engagement. I personally try to limit their use to those areas of Lean Thinking where the word is either in the common vocabulary, such as Kaizen, or where I feel that it is important to explain the difference between the Lean approach that it describes and its local language translation. Kamishibai is one such word. While its English translation, 'layered audit', is not incorrect, I feel that the word audit implies the traditional approach of a 'poacher and gamekeeper' relationship between the auditor and audited.

Instead, I use the word Kamishibai to describe its place in Visible Leadership, whereby the Lean Leader uses this simple but structured approach to interact with team members, coaching and embodying the role of Leader as a Teacher, one of the Lean Leadership paradigms. The approach of Kamishibai is covered in more detail in Chapter 12, Coaching Leadership, the important element being that Visible Leadership gives real meaning to the interactions with the team members, driving sustained and continuous improvement of the Lean System in the organisation. A colleague of mine describes it as the 'glue of the Lean Operating System' because it is the way in which the leadership conveys the importance of standardisation and adherence to those standards, as well as ensuring compliance.

The most important thing about Kamishibai is its differences from a traditional audit: it is regular, small-scale, leader-led and focussed on rapid problem solving and improvement (Kaizen) in a short period of time. Above all, it is about checking the process, not the person, and building the visibility of the Lean Leader in the Visual Showcase that is created during the Lean Transformation.

Visible Leadership is essential for a Lean Organisation and it alone can be the Critical Success Factor for the essential act of engaging our people in the Lean Transformation. If you're interested in reading more about this, *The Lean Turnaround* by Art Byrne[2] has some great examples of how he has been a Visible Leader throughout his successful leadership career.

HANSEI

Before moving onto the next chapter, please take a few moments to reflect. When it comes to your own way of working, what are:

1. Your key learning points?

....

....

....

....

2. The changes that you could make?

....

....

....

....

3. Current problems that they would help to solve?

....

....

....

....

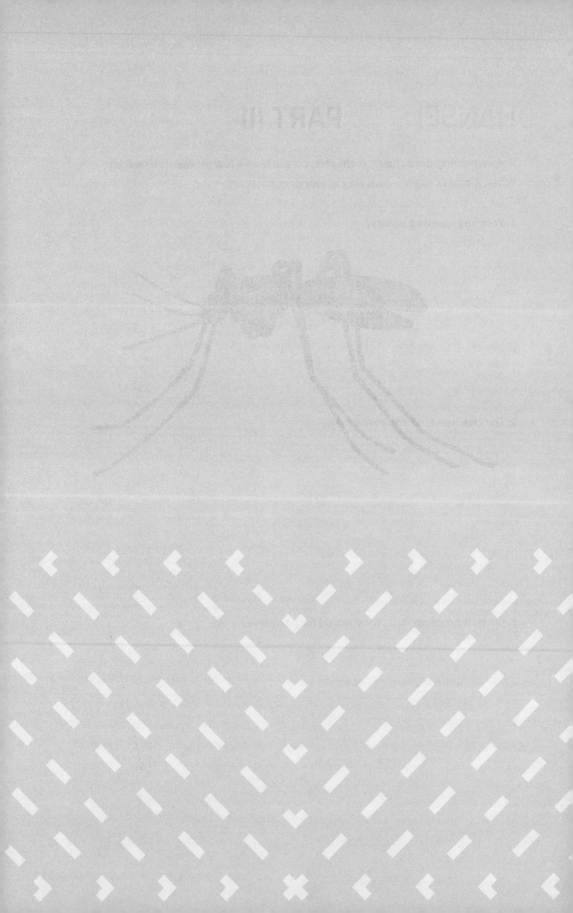

PART III
LEADING AT SCALE

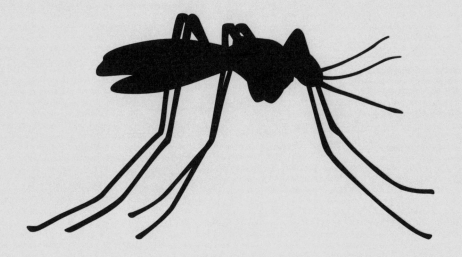

10. LEARNING FROM SUCCESS

The Kaikaku experience

The word Kaizen is part of the vocabulary of most people in modern business and I would certainly expect the readership of this book to be very familiar with its meaning (literally a 'change for good') and with the Kaizen culture of Lean Enterprises that the vast majority of organisations attempt to emulate.

A closely related term in the Japanese Lean lexicon is Kaikaku, which literally translated means 'radical change' and is the part of improvement where changes are made to the business that would not be achieved through the smaller incremental steps of Kaizen. Neither Kaizen or Kaikaku are better than the other and, in fact, both are required if we are to be successful in our transformation; building a Kaizen culture whereby every member of our organisation makes sustainable improvement every day (Kaizen), whilst highly effective project teams and Kaizen event teams create step-change improvements on a less frequent, but still regular, basis (Kaikaku).

These complementary approaches are absolutely essential if we are to see our enterprise reach its targets and must be embraced in the Lean Transformation.

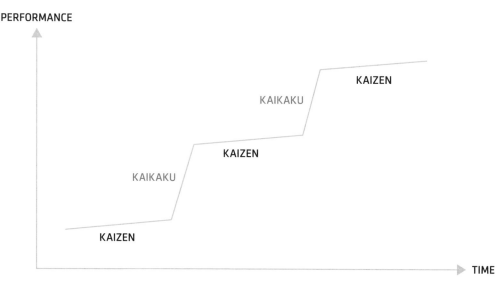

The complementary approaches of Kaikaku and Kaizen

This concept of Kaikaku must also be applied in learning from success, as we need to get out there and set our vision of the future, our Kaikaku vision, and to do this we need to go and see (go to Gemba) other companies who are significantly ahead of us in terms of their Lean Transformation. This doesn't need to be those organisations who are truly at the level of a Lean Enterprise, such as Toyota, but can be organisations who are a few years ahead of our Lean Transformation.

The general rule is that you must see things there that both simultaneously excite and scare you, as they are both highly appealing as a vision of what you want to achieve and realistic to envision but, at the same time, you have a certain fear of the challenges ahead to achieve it.

In my own experience, I recall visiting companies, such as Ricoh, Omron and Parker Hannifin, where they had effective pull systems supported by great daily management and problem solving and an enviable Kaizen culture. These 'visual factories' seemed light years ahead of the Philips Consumer Lifestyle factories where I was responsible for Lean Deployment.

However, as a leadership team we took inspiration from those visits (and many others) and grasped the challenge that they presented. Fast forward to the present and every one of those Consumer Lifestyle factories has reached a level comparable to those that we visited around seven years ago, with two of them having won World Class Manufacturing Awards. They are all now regularly visited by external parties who want to experience a 'Kaikaku vision' themselves.

It is therefore an essential part of setting the vision that the leadership visits other organisations that will both inspire and challenge them to make significant change during their own Lean Transformation. If not, the risk is that the goals for the transformation will be simply too modest, as they are potentially stuck in unconscious incompetence (they don't know what they don't know - Chapter 4) and are unable to picture a future significantly different from their current state.

It's not industrial tourism

The visiting of these enterprises to gain the vision of excellence is often called the 'Kaikaku experience' and an important element of the experience is that it should not become 'industrial tourism' but must be a true opportunity for the leadership to experience what their future could look like.

To achieve this, the Lean Leader must follow some basic but important rules when designing the Kaikaku experience for their leadership team:

1. **Preparation:**

The Lean Leader must ensure that they create a network of external contacts across a number of organisations based upon a mixture of the industry that they are in, the areas of the business in which they are deploying Lean and the maturity of their Lean Transformation. In some cases these relationships will be established on a transactional basis, whereby access to 'go see' is a commercial arrangement, as can be found with Toyota and other larger organisations with world-class credentials.

Similarly, there are several consultancies who can organise Kaikaku experiences in most parts of the world and there are many who will take you, for a price, to the source and the ultimate opportunity to go see the Japanese Kaikaku experience.

These types of commercial arrangement can be extremely useful but with the caveat that the Lean Leader must still do due diligence and ensure that the visits will be suitable for their organisation's leadership team to see what they need for inspiration and challenge. This does not mean that they should only look for companies that do exactly the same as they do, but it does mean that the businesses to be visited will have elements of a business system that could address some of the biggest problems facing their company. Whilst transactional arrangements can be useful for arranging Kaikaku experiences, building mutually beneficial relationships with other organisations can be equally fruitful. The difficulty with this is that you want to visit organisations that are more advanced than yours in their Lean Transformation and therefore the quid pro quo becomes more challenging. What can you offer them in return for their time and effort in hosting you? In some cases you may each have elements of your transformation that are better than the other's. For example you may have a great learning academy in place, while they've done more in terms of instigating daily management and problem solving. In other cases it could be that you've got something else to offer, such as providing them with facilities to use for meetings and workshops or maybe your marketing director is an expert in online marketing and can spend some time speaking to their marketing team.

You may find that some companies simply value your external view and ability to provide them with some independent feedback. This has been one element that my colleagues and I have used, especially as we've developed a network of visited companies and can provide subjective feedback to those that we visit, while of course respecting the confidentiality of those companies that we have previously visited.

The Lean Leader will get to know the potential Kaikaku experience organisations very well and understand how they can be best utilised overall for their own organisation's learning but also specifically for different parts of their organisation, for example for the new product development, marketing or manufacturing teams. They will maintain a catalogue of the enterprises and will design the Kaikaku experiences as much as possible around the match between the participants' learning needs and the available plethora of companies.

The obvious caveat here is that there is a finite number of times that each company may be visited, especially where the relationship is based on contact and mutual learning as opposed to commercial interchange. Additionally, for a global organisation, there will be geographical, cultural and language challenges to manage. This means that the Lean Leader must build as large a database as is possible to ensure that the Kaikaku experience needs of the organisation may be met over time.

2. **Facilitation:**

To facilitate the visits in the right spirit, it's essential that the Lean Leader creates something that is truly an experience. A typical Kaikaku experience will include visits to between two and four companies, with three being an effective number for learning. These companies will all demonstrate something a little different for the participants and could be a mix of manufacturing and knowledge companies. One such trip that we previously used was Toyota (car assembly), Ricoh (printing machines) and Virgin Money (credit cards). The visited companies should be as geographically close as possible to allow for a tour that is not overly burdened by travel and allows the travel to be arranged in a way that builds the team experience, such as hiring a motor coach to take the team together. The team visit will then be focussed on attending the Kaikaku experience together and having a shared learning experience.

The participants will receive a Kaikaku experience brochure ahead of the visit, which will explain the objectives of the visit, the background of the companies to be visited and the learning expectations per company. This document will have been well researched by the Lean Leader as part of their preparation for the Kaikaku tour.

During the tour, the Lean Leader will facilitate the group as their coach and will assign learning tasks to the team members to ensure that the visits have real meaning, with the objectives understood by the participants and fulfilled. To do this, the Lean Leader will follow an agenda that ensures that the tour is effective:

- Take one day per company visit to avoid being rushed.
- Manage travel time to allow at least four hours at each company, ensuring sufficient time to learn.
- Incorporate a briefing and debriefing per visit, to ensure that the participants are prepared before visiting and reflect and capture their learning immediately afterwards.

An example of a typical visit agenda for one company would therefore be:

08:00   Breakfast briefing:
-   Overview of the company to be visited
-   A reminder of the visit etiquette
-   Confirmation of the team learning objectives
-   Assignment of the learning focus for each team member

09:00   Arrive at company X, registration and safety briefing

09:30   Introductions to hosts, sharing of visit objectives by both parties

10:00   Go to Gemba - Part 1

12:00   Working lunch - General discussions with the hosts

12:45   Go to Gemba - Part 2

14:00   Q&A session, wrap-up, thank you to the hosts
(including a gift within company policy) and farewells

15:00   End of visit

15:30   Debriefing session:
-   Reflections of the visit
-   Capture the general and team-member-specific learning
-   Determine the immediate knowledge transfers of own Lean Deployment

17:00   End of day and travel

An important part of the visit etiquette is the maintenance of the mindset around learning and not criticising. While it is valid to ask questions for clarification, especially where a particular approach has been used and it is unclear to a participant why it was done that way, the intent must be to learn and not to try to prove that the hosts are not doing it well enough.

Depending on how the visit is progressing and the relationship built between the Lean Leader and the host company's people, the hosts may ask for feedback and be open to advice or criticism. However, this should always be given in good faith and with the intent of shared learning and discovery. Nothing will irrevocably damage the relationship between the continuous improvement teams of two companies faster than the feeling that one of the parties is trying to prove a superiority of knowledge.

Instead, the best advice that I can ever give to the participants of a Kaikaku experience, or to be honest most visits to other enterprises, is to constantly look for great ideas to learn from and utilise in their own organisation, what I jokingly refer to as 'proudly stealing'.

3. **Post-visit:**

After the visit the participants, the leadership of the particular areas of the business beginning their Lean Transformation, will spend further time determining how the learning from their Kaikaku experience may be best incorporated into their organisation. They will have seen and experienced much and, whilst a 'cut and paste' approach is often not possible, there should be a great deal of inspiration for improvements in their ways of working and these must be grasped with both hands.

The Lean Leader again plays a key role in this part of the process, ensuring that the follow-up happens and that the learning is translated into tangible activity. Where ideas cannot yet be adopted, possibly due to it being simply too early, they should be properly captured for posterity and regularly reviewed.

The model line as the internal Kaikaku experience

In the early days of the Lean Deployment, external parties will need to be used for the Kaikaku experiences, simply because the organisation will not have any areas of its own to showcase. However, as its transformation progresses, model lines will be created, which can become internal Kaikaku sites and their use should be encouraged.

However, just as with the external sites, they must be used with meaning and industrial tourism avoided. Especially in the early days, when there are only a few of them, they will be in high demand and it is therefore essential that visits are managed by the Lean Leader and the model line leadership to avoid overload. The model lines must therefore be managed as part of the Kaikaku experience database and planning process.

The use of external companies should be ongoing, even when the transformation is at a high level of maturity, as external benchmarking and learning must be continual. In fact, probably the best way to utilise the internal sites is as one of the Kaikaku experience visit locations and therefore the visits become a mixture of both internal and external organisations.

One of the biggest advantages of having internal models of excellence is the ease with which others in the organisation will accept that Lean will work for them, as it is much more difficult to say, 'Yes, I see that it works for Virgin, Toyota and Honeywell but we don't provide credit cards, make cars or instrument clusters' when the organisation is doing the same thing.

Another key advantage of having internal Kaikaku sites is that the host's people work for the same company and speak the same business language, work in the same (or a very similar) culture, face similar problems and have common (high-level) goals. This makes it much easier for the participants of the visit and their hosts to create the connections

that support effective communication and enable successful knowledge transfer.
If these physical visits can be augmented and replicated virtually, through the use of
internal social media sites, webcasts, videos and newsletters, this knowledge sharing and
replication can be scaled up and the viral effect created (discussed further in Mosquito
Leadership in Chapter 11) that will infect the organisation with good ideas. However, to
do so the Lean Leader must tackle the syndrome of 'not-invented-here' effectively.

Not-invented-here syndrome

'Not-invented-here' syndrome is one of the biggest disablers of effective learning and
knowledge transfer that exists. It is a natural human attitude to resist the idea that
someone else's way-of-working could be better than one's own and will result, at best, in
a reinvention of the wheel and, at worst, in completely missing the opportunity to adopt
best practice.
In the best case scenario, the team will essentially adopt the idea but, instead of taking it and adapting it to work in their organisation, they will completely reengineer it,
including rewriting standard work instructions in their own parlance. To some extent this
can be part of the change management process, as the team internalise and make the
idea their own, which can help with ownership and the sustainability of the approach.
However, this must be kept to a minimum if the organisation is to become a learning
organisation and rapidly adopt new ways of working without excessive time spend in
implementation.
In the worst case scenario, the team rejects best practices as inappropriate for their
organisation and creates a form of organisational allergy to outside influences. This is
a change management issue, as it is deeply rooted in the fear of change and must be
overcome if the organisation is to take advantage of the many best practices that exist
outside their immediate domain. As discussed in Chapter 3, there are some important
change leadership tactics that must be employed, described by Kotter's eight steps of
change leadership. The Lean Deployment approach must ensure that the team members start to address some of their key fears of change and learn to see the advantages
for them, answering the question 'What's in it for me?' that is critical to gaining their
engagement in the transformation.
The 'not-invented-here' mindset is not always obvious and its symptoms can manifest
themselves as perceived stubbornness or incompetence as the team fails to reap the
benefits that were observed in the Kaikaku organisation. However, the Lean Thinking
Leader understands that nothing is as simple as it appears at face value and will take the
time to understand why intelligent and experienced team members are failing to gain

the benefits so seemingly obvious to everyone else. It is only when this understanding is applied that this significant barrier may be removed.

Scale, scale, scale

Wherever the best practices are discovered or developed, either internally or externally, it is critical that they are scaled as quickly as possible to gain the coverage across the organisation that we need. As discussed in the previous section, avoiding 'not-invented-here' syndrome requires careful change leadership and so scaling cannot be done in a mechanical fashion. As Peter Senge[1] famously said:

> *People don't resist change, they resist being changed*

It is therefore crucial that the Lean Leader attains balance between the speed of scaling through a 'cut-and-paste' technique, convincing the team members to adopt the ideas by giving them ownership of the approach. This is one of the key elements of the VIRAL model, discussed in Chapter 5, whereby the replication stage takes those best practices, the new standard work, and replicates them across the whole organisation.

This approach to replication ensures that the model lines, created in Stage 2, have adopted as many external best practices as possible and have effectively implemented the Kaikaku as well as Kaizen improvements. This ensures that the replication across the organisation can take place with the reassurance for the receiving teams that these ways of working are applicable to their organisation and are not just external best practices being imposed upon them dogmatically.

This doesn't remove the necessity for the receiving team to adopt the new ways of working through a process that earns their ownership. It does, however, reduce the reinvention, as the Why and What of the methodologies should be clear and the time invested goes on the How. As the whole organisation gains experience in effective learning, it will become a core competency and a continuous part of the team's modus operandi. This must be supported with a knowledge management system that enables rapid and effective knowledge sharing amongst the teams, particularly those that are geographically dispersed, and a Kaizen system that allows rapid improvements in a culture of continuous improvement while still protecting the standardisation required across all team members undertaking the same activity. This means that the problem of who approves Kaizen and when they can be implemented needs to be solved and in Chapter 17 I will discuss how to reconcile the local and value stream approach which can cause this to be a challenge.

Whilst the pursuit of perfection is essential to the Lean Leader, not yet having the perfect knowledge management and Kaizen systems in place should not be a barrier to replication and scale-up. The environment you will have come from will most likely be one that had a lack of adherence to standard work and infrequent improvement and so the tension created by having imperfect Kaizen and knowledge management systems is a small price to pay for the improvement in ways of working.

HANSEI

Before moving onto the next chapter, please take a few moments to reflect.
When it comes to your own way of working, what are:

1. Your key learning points?

2. The changes that you could make?

3. Current problems that they would help to solve?

11. GOING VIRAL - MOSQUITO LEADERSHIP

The Lean virus

In Chapters 7 and 9 I discussed Leadership Activism and Visible Leadership, two forms of Leadership that the Lean Leader must practise. Following on from these is the third form of Leadership in the repertoire of the Lean Leader: Mosquito Leadership.

Most readers will have a certain familiarity with the concept of spreading ideas, news or opinions 'virally' and despite the fact that very few, if any, of us would like to catch a real virus, we are happy to catch many of the viral trends that are out there.

Extending the analogy, the Mosquito Leadership style is one where the Lean Leader spreads the change in mindset virally by 'infecting' the organisation with their ideas and beliefs. Again, this is complementary to the other leadership styles and so the Leadership Activism and Visibility covered in earlier chapters play a significant part in this.

The philosophy behind this form of leadership is that a leader is not limited in influence and impact by job title, role description or hierarchal position. Instead, they identify the long-term impact that they wish to have on their organisation and develop a strategy to make it happen. The name given to this form of leadership was inspired by a traditional African proverb:

> *If you think that you are too small to make a difference,*
> *try sleeping in a closed room with a mosquito.*

This is precisely why this form of leadership is so important to being an effective Lean Leader, as without the willingness to go out and infect colleagues, the critical mass of change required for a Lean Transformation and the pursuit of excellence will not be achieved.

The Lean Leader understands that their sphere of control is relatively small, even when they have risen to a quite senior level in their organisation. However, they know that their success depends upon increasing their sphere of influence far beyond that which they would normally derive from the position that they hold and they strive energetically to increase its diameter every day.

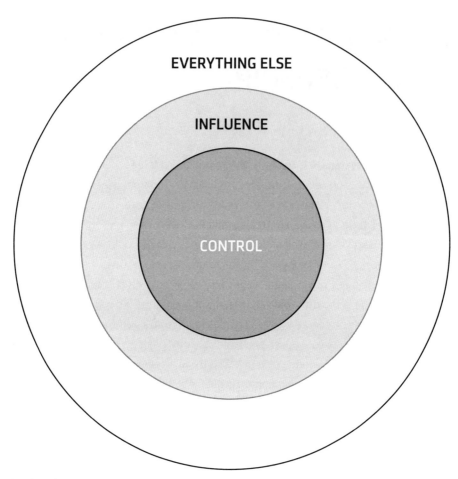

The sphere of control

There are multiple ways in which they can do this but, at the core is a belief in what they want to achieve and a willingness to create the networks required to achieve it. In the digital era we now live in, this is much easier in terms of the media available. Social media in particular have enabled the Lean Leader to increase their sphere of influence beyond those people that they meet in person and reach a global audience.

Whilst external sites like LinkedIn are great tools for this, internal social media sites, such as those provided by Socialcast[1], and the use of webinars and webcasts, are excellent ways to engage with the organisation directly and to ensure that their voice is heard. Many large organisations now have these media available for use and the Lean Leader must include them in the change and communication plans of their transformation and ensure that these communication channels are utilised in a smart way for the various stakeholders.

One of the great things about the social media platforms is the opportunity to create a dialogue, rather than one-way communication, as is the case with media such as newsletters, webcasts or email. Just as with LinkedIn, or other applications such as Facebook or Twitter, a discussion can take place amongst all subscribers, allowing questions to be asked and answered, ideas shared and contributions made by people not originally in the target audience. Coupled with this is the additional advantage that spontaneous messaging and sharing by subscribers across the organisation can be precipitated through a consistent use of the site and encouragement and recognition for those brave few who contribute.

Nevertheless, while social media have increased the opportunities to engage with a larger audience, this has not diminished the personal courage required by the Lean Leader to do so. This is because this form of communication does not require, or in fact warrant, a traditional communication approach whereby leaders employ the services of communication managers to draft communications, proofreading and editing them before publication. Instead the Lean Leader will author the vast majority of their own messages. Whilst a few carefully crafted missives will remain part of the communication plan, they will constitute a small percentage. The majority of the messaging will be short, frequent and unsophisticated, where the Lean Leader will share their thoughts and experiences personally and openly with the organisation through internal social media.

This means that the Lean Leader will demonstrate a level of vulnerability, as they open themselves up and share not only their successes but also their failures and they may even err in some of the messaging. However, this honesty, whilst possibly seen as weakness by those few team members resistant to change, will build trust and respect with the majority of the organisation.

The beliefs of the Mosquito Leader

To adopt the Mosquito Leadership style certain beliefs must be held by the Lean Leader, which will allow them to work in a manner that takes them outside of a traditional hierarchal structure. While these beliefs will, by definition, be personal to the individual, the true Lean Leader is one who is highly capable of executing the transformation strategy and has an ethos based on fundamental principles along the following lines:

1. If I truly believe in the vision, mission and values of the organisation in which I operate, I must be a leader in the change required to realise our goals.
2. However, I am not a lone soldier or a maverick; I am an agent for change.
3. I know that I deliver more when I focus on we.

4. I realise that I don't have all the answers, in fact I have only a few, but I'll find the people who collectively do have them.
5. Whilst my legacy may be small in terms of human history, it will be significant in the area on which I'm focussed.
6. Only my discipline and focus will be an equal to my stamina.
7. I will only regret the mistakes that I made by not doing what I believed was right; all other mistakes I will simply learn and improve from.
8. I am the culture of my organisation, not the victim of it, and I will never blame it for my failure to deliver or let it prevent me from doing what must be done.
9. I do this because it is the right thing to do for the organisation, not for career advancement.

These beliefs power the success of the Mosquito Leadership approach, as they create faith in the approach and fuel the content of the communication method. The Lean Leader's belief in leading the change to achieve the vision, mission and values of the organisation will motivate them to share their intentions for the organisation's transformation. They will create clear, visible messaging to share around the company.

Similarly, their belief in the need to collectively answer the organisation's problems will stimulate them to create dialogue across the organisation and this dialogue will, in turn, recruit others into the conversation. The conviction of the Lean Leader in learning from mistakes will ensure that they have the confidence to share all of their experiences, which will motivate others to overcome their fear and try this new way of working.

Belief Number 8 is a particularly powerful element of the Lean Leader's psyche, as they do not allow the culture of the organisation to be an excuse for failure, understanding that the culture of the organisation is the sum of the behaviours and mindsets of all of the team members. They know that they have the power to refuse to behave in the way that the current culture might demand and instead to behave in a way that is in accordance with the culture that the organisation wants to attain. This attitude of embodying the culture that you want pervades the messages, both verbal and visual, that the Lean Leader transmits to the organisation.

The faith and beliefs held by the Lean Leader will be clear to some of the organisation in the short term and to all of the organisation in the longer term. It is therefore essential that the Lean Leader is genuine if they are to create the virus that will infect the organisation and unleash it through their adoption of Mosquito Leadership. Disingenuousness will be detected sooner or later and any credibility will be consigned to the dustbin. Therefore, before making the first proverbial bite in the organisation, it is essential that the Lean Leader has clearly defined their beliefs and why they are doing what they aim to do. By doing this, they can ensure that they have met the first of the required beliefs, their faith in the organisation's vision, mission and values, providing credibility in the philosophy that they want to infect the organisation with.

Influence beyond hierarchy

In case the metaphor of the mosquito has engendered the idea that the Mosquito Leader is a nuisance within the organisation and someone to be eradicated, let me assure readers that the Mosquito Leader is not an agent fighting against the organisation but, instead, someone who believes passionately in the goals of the business. They are highly engaged in challenging the business to meet those goals better, more effectively and with greater success than they otherwise would.

They are certainly a disruptive influence, but in a very positive sense, as they constantly ask difficult questions of the organisation and expect the status quo to be seen as something that will soon enter into history. Whilst the mosquito often carries the malaria virus, which humans try to avoid, the organisation will gain greatly from the virus that the Mosquito Leader will infect it with, one of transformation.

Mosquito Leadership is not easy, as it requires that the person is prepared to step out of their comfort zone and expand on their normal duties. They may find, in fact will often find, resistance from across the organisation and will not find favour with those who fear the change that they are advocating and are activist in bringing about. In this sense they will be an irritant, just like the mosquito, but it is a necessary part of this type of leadership, whereby they must:

> *Inspire through their actions; challenge fear of change with their heart and mind; execute through their discipline, focus and stamina.*

The true Mosquito Leader, as they grow in their role as a thought leader and role model for change, will deliver a persistent legacy, significant in their organisation, which they, and everyone involved, can be extremely proud of.

HANSEI

Before moving onto the next chapter, please take a few moments to reflect.
When it comes to your own way of working, what are:

1. Your key learning points?

....

....

....

....

2. The changes that you could make?

....

....

....

....

3. Current problems that they would help to solve?

....

....

....

....

12. COACHING LEADERSHIP

Hansei

From an early age, Japanese Children learn what the Japanese call 'Hansei', a form of self-reflection to understand what went wrong in a given situation and to learn from it. From their first social interactions at kindergarten, when a Japanese child behaves in a way deemed unacceptable to their teacher, they will be asked to take some Hansei time to think about what they have done wrong, then explain their reflections to their teacher and what they might do differently in the future.

Whilst it could be argued that children are often asked to 'think about what you've done' in Western society, it is much more common for the child to be told what it is that they did wrong and how they should adjust their behaviour to conform in the future. This differs from the approach taken with the Japanese school child.

The habit of Hansei is probably one of the key differences between the Japanese and Western way of thinking. This may go some way toward explaining why problem solving in the form of the Deming or PDCA Cycle was adopted with such sustainability by a large number of Japanese companies and resonates at every level in the organisation, from practical problem solving at the shop-floor level through to Hoshin Kanri at the board level.

This way of reflecting and improving one's performance, effectively personal practice of the check and act parts of the cycle, is central to Coaching Leadership, the fourth and final leadership style of the Lean Leader. The Lean Leader must be able to both practise and teach Hansei in order to garner the level of deep reflection that the Lean Organisation requires. When the Lean Leader is able to practise Hansei as a habit, a certain freedom of action is achieved, whereby they feel free to experiment with new approaches and accept challenges without the fear of failure. It is a liberating experience.

My personal experience with Hansei started around seven years ago, when I learned of the practice and decided to experiment with it. To say that it was a personal revolution in my effectiveness is not hyperbole and I cannot stress enough its importance to a Lean Leader. Whilst I already had in place some of the habits that make Hansei effective, capturing my daily thoughts and meeting notes both in writing and diagrammatically, the discipline of taking time out of my day to think and reflect on what went well and what didn't and to critically determine how to improve was a revelation.

The approach that I now take is simultaneously simple and difficult to do. At the end of every day I have half an hour of Hansei time planned, in which I reflect upon and review the day to determine what went well, what didn't and, from each, what I learnt and how

I can act differently in the future. Whilst that in itself is simple, the difficulty lies in the reality that the most challenging days are those on which it is most difficult to find the time to spend on Hansei, as they are the ones where one feels most compelled to do more and not to 'waste time' reflecting.

Despite this challenge, I have found that by forcing myself to invest the time, I have been able to learn and improve my ways of working. I feel that this has made a great improvement in my personal performance and, ultimately, my articles on LinkedIn and this book have been born out of my Hansei moments.

However, despite the importance of developing this Hansei approach, the Lean Leader's greatest challenge is to establish this practice in others. This is difficult in a traditional organisation as, despite the widely accepted knowledge of the four Situational Leadership styles [1] of Directive, Supporting, Coaching and Delegating, Leadership is predominantly associated with the Directive style. Often the expectation, from both the leader and those led, is that the solution to a problem will be given by the leader and that the team member will simply follow their instruction and implement.

This approach is addictive, as both the leader and the team member gain a certain security. The leader feels like they have done something and the team member's risk level is relatively low; if it works they will be rewarded and if it doesn't it wasn't their idea. However, the simple fact is that this creates a culture whereby the team members become dependent on the leader to solve all of the problems and very little is done without the leader's input, decision or direction. This results in only a few of the most urgent, but not necessarily most important, problems being solved, leaving many problems persistently unsolved, and hence multiple opportunities untapped.

It is therefore essential that the Lean Leader changes the approach with their team members and that of the other leaders in the organisation, by taking an approach that encourages the team members to reflect on problems and solve them without being told what to do, instead employing their own knowledge, intelligence and experience.

Toyota Kata

An approach that is prevalent in Toyota, and has hence been termed 'Toyota Kata', as documented by Mike Rother,[2] works on the basis of 'Genchi Genbutsu' (or going to where the work is done) and is aimed at creating an interaction between the leader and the team member that is based upon mutual respect and the inherent pursuit of creating sustainable solutions and learning for both.

The approach is very simple to understand but takes discipline and, for most managers, a change in leadership approach and style as they practise helping their people to find solutions through a coaching, rather than a directive style of leadership.

The Lean Leader will, as a visible leader, be at the workplace regularly and be interacting with their team members to support their daily management of the operations (whether that be a manufacturing floor, design office or marketing suite) and will take the time to understand how the organisation is performing and where problems need to be solved. A great way to do this is to ask questions and, through an approach called 'Kamishibai' (discussed in Chapter 9) the leader can visit their people with meaning, rather than to 'tick a box'.

The Kamishibai approach is a 'layered audit' of a process or step thereof and is named after a Japanese story-telling approach that is used with children to tell a story visually. The name was adopted because the approach uses visual cards to determine which process the 'auditor' should check, the questions to be asked and the result.

An example of Kamishibai cards

The philosophy of the approach is that by doing many of them but on a small scale, more problems will be solved and increased ownership will be encouraged compared with a traditional audit approach, which typically is larger in scale, uses auditors external to the department and is usually undertaken in the spirit of 'poacher and gamekeeper'. As with all Lean Thinking, the Kamishibai is essentially about localised ownership, short-interval control, visual management and rapid problem solving.

The Lean Leader will therefore use Kamishibai to integrate Kata into the organisation and, as it matures, peer as well as leadership Kamishibai will develop, as the team members start to check each other's processes and help each other to improve every day. Of course, the key element in all of this is that trust is developed and that the team members understand and believe that the check is performed on the process and not on them.

Whilst the questions asked when employing Kata can be developed by the team members, the best starting point, and what has become almost the Kata Standard, is to ask the following:

1. What is the target condition?
2. What is the actual condition now?
3. Which obstacles do you think are preventing you from achieving the target condition now?
4. What is your next step? What do you expect?
4. How quickly will we be able to see the outcome of that step?

By asking these questions, the Lean Leader may develop an understanding, along with the team member, of how the process is performing and where problems can be solved. Most importantly, this enables the leader to coach the team members to solve the problem for themselves. When this is undertaken successfully, it will gradually embolden the associates to take the ownership and accountability to do this not only when they are being challenged and coached by their leaders but on a daily basis themselves, when they see the problems that they would previously have ignored or accepted.

Of course, the Kata approach should not be reserved exclusively for during the Kamishibai activity, as it is equally valid during times of problem solving with the team members. However, the Kamishibai is a great way of proactively uncovering issues that may remain persistently unresolved due a perception that they are unimportant to the leadership. In fact, through this activity, Leadership Activism is demonstrated to the team members and the importance of 'Kaizen everyday', the solving of small problems on a daily basis, is both modelled and reinforced.

The final leadership style

This leadership style, Coaching Leadership, is the fourth and final style required for 'Leading with Lean' and is integral to the Lean Leadership approach.

To illustrate this, imagine how frustrating it must be as the coach of a football (soccer) team during the game; at worst they see their carefully drawn-up game plan evaporate in front of their very eyes and, at best, they may win but have to watch as not everything goes to plan and they rely on their players to make changes to the play as they respond to the actions of the opposition.

They can, of course, try to speak to their players whilst they are playing and it's not unusual to observe coaches who arrived at the game cool and collected screaming incessantly at their players during the game. However, no matter how much coaches try to influence their players with their cries from the sideline, the crucial point is that they are not on the field of play and the game is played by the players themselves.

While the coach may have an overwhelming urge to enter the field of play, they have the advantage of being prohibited by the laws of the game and therefore have no choice but to coach from the sidelines. This is an advantage because, if they were allowed to enter the field of play, they may try to do the work for the players but would, inevitably, only make things worse and demotivate the team.

Relating this back to business, far too often leaders micromanage their team members, entering the field of play and trying to play the game for them. However, ironically, the supposed problem solving is usually not done at the Gemba but in a meeting room or remote office, using online dashboards, discussing perceptions of problems and opinions on solutions, which far too often do not include the insight or expertise of the people who actually do the work. Instead, a new mandate, set of golden rules or procedures are sent to those who do the work, providing them with the 'answer' to a problem they didn't know existed and which doesn't address the root cause(s) of the issues that they face every day.

The result is the dichotomy of a system that combines over-intimate management, including firefighting on a daily basis, with remote problem solving, leading to demotivated and frustrated team members and, at best, average operational performance.

As Steve Jobs once said:

It doesn't make sense to hire smart people and then tell them what to do; we hire smart people so that they can tell us what to do.

Learning from the laws of the game of football (and most sports), there is the need to build a system whereby the Leaders of the organisation focus their work on setting its vision, mission, values and strategic objectives. Then, by working with their teams, they convert the objectives into goals with clear deliverables that are cascaded throughout the organisation and, through the training and development of their staff, build the overall organisational capability that will support the creation of a high-performance culture.

Crucially, they must allow their people to do the work and problem solve, without telling them what to do. This is not to say that leaders should be banned from going to the Gemba; quite the contrary, as we want them there more than they currently are on average, as discussed in the chapters on the Visible and Activist Leadership styles, but what we need is for them to coach, not try to play the game for their team.

This requires a different skillset and mindset than most leaders have developed over their careers, changing their role from the most experienced and expert of the team (or at least thinking that), able to tell everyone how to fix the problems, to a coaching role, asking the right questions to enable the team to solve their problems structurally. Most importantly, they need to allow their people to make mistakes and learn from them, approaching the solution and doing things differently than they would personally prefer. This is a key component of Lean Leadership, as it is the only way that an individual can have the scale of impact that is necessary to drive high business performance, getting results through enabling the skills of others and their engagement in the work, as opposed to by telling them what to do. This requires a leap of faith from the individual leader, facing a perceived loss of control and a fear that performance will go downhill without their explicit intervention and direction.

Whilst it is true that if control has been the norm in the organisation or group then a complete change overnight is not advisable, as the team will not have the requisite organisational capability, the change in behaviour and ways of working has to begin and make significant progress while we build the capability and trust of the team.

Moving to a Coaching Leadership style will not be easy. However, it is essential to achieve long-term sustainable success for the organisation.

The journey to a Coaching Style

Earlier in the Chapter I referred to the four situational leadership styles of Directive, Supporting, Coaching and Delegating and how traditional leadership is predominantly associated with the Directive style. The journey to a Coaching style therefore depends upon the leadership actively practising the different styles and managing the change of behaviour in the organisation. This will be difficult, as at every level of the organisation people will find this difficult for one reason or another, depending on their personal motivations.

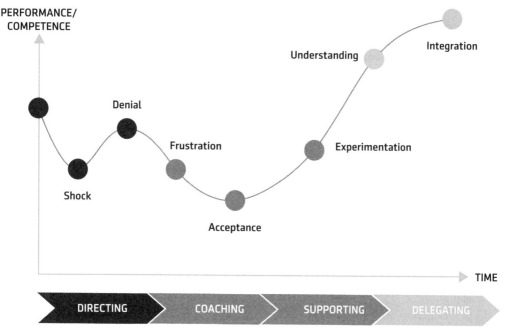

The change curve and situational leadership

For some leaders, especially middle managers, this will be perceived as a challenge to their raison d'être, as the change in their way of working, actively coaching their team members toward autonomy, will provide uncertainty about their role in the organisation. If the teams become autonomous, what is the need for them?

For others it might cause them to question their role as manager of the group or department, as their passion may actually lie in the technical role itself, what they studied and trained to do, and so a general management role that appears to encourage them to keep out of the technical elements of the job might be unappealing.

For some team members this move to autonomy could be seen as adding responsibility to their role and could be perceived as increasing the risk of their role, without visible benefits. As discussed earlier in the book, answering the question 'What's in it for me?' is especially pertinent for this cohort.

Despite these concerns, the truth is that the organisation's journey through the performance and associated change curve will not result in a reduced requirement for middle managers (group leaders, area managers and department heads). In fact there will be an increased need for these leaders of operational excellence, the people who set the vision of success for their people and establish the enablers for their success.

Their functional expertise will be required more than ever but they will be required to act as teachers to those less able than themselves, creating a virtuous cycle of learning as the leader learns by teaching. In fact the power of this is that the team members and the leader start to build upon each other's ideas and successes as the learning becomes self-perpetuating.

For the team members, the fear of autonomy increasing the risk profile of their role is ill-founded, as it actually allows them to take far more control of their job and its future direction than they have ever had before, as they gain the opportunity to implement the ideas that they have held for a long time and to solve the problems that cause frustration every day.

In fact, for those team members in high-cost countries, the case for cost reduction through the transfer of their work to lower-cost locations or its automation can be challenged and in some cases prevented through the eradication of the waste in the process and the achievement of operational excellence. This is because the case for wage arbitrage reduces when wasteful activity is removed, as the value proposition of the value-added part of the process is often much more focussed on the service and quality elements than cost. In the case of automation, once waste has been reduced significantly, the added flexibility of a human being can refocus the organisation toward higher value-added propositions as opposed to efficiency-based approaches. Examples of this have been documented with Mercedes Benz and Virgin Money.

The journey from the directive style to the coaching style of leadership will not be an easy one, as there are many changes in mindset to effect. However, it is an essential part of Leading with Lean and, starting with themselves, the Lean Leader will have to ensure that it is a key part of the change leadership of their organisation's Lean Transformation.

HANSEI

Before moving onto the next chapter, please take a few moments to reflect.
When it comes to your own way of working, what are:

1. Your key learning points?

....

....

....

....

2. The changes that you could make?

....

....

....

....

3. Current problems that they would help to solve?

....

....

....

....

13. THE BUSINESS EXCELLENCE COMPETITION

The Philips Excellence Competition

In September 2015 I completed 10 years working for Royal Philips, which gave me pause to reflect on some fantastic experiences and shared achievements during this time. However, despite the many sources of pride that I have as a team member of Philips, one of the most engaging is the Philips Excellence Competition (PEC).

Whilst there are many companies that celebrate the success of their business excellence initiatives, Philips must surely be one of an elite club of organisations who, on an annual basis, invest in a global celebration of their team members' achievements. It is called the Philips Excellence Competition and it is open to all of the 100K+ employees across the globe.[1] Although it is a competition, and does bring out the competitive nature of the Philips team members, the real magic of the PEC is the opportunity to engage all employees in the important matter of excellence. The competition runs company-wide, across the whole value chain and its enabling functions, from our teams in research all the way through to after-sales care. The competition celebrates the essence of Philips, delivering 'innovation that matters to you', its customers, and ensures that the best ideas are not only rewarded but are shared across the whole of the Philips world.

That year's competition brought those teams who had beaten the best of their market and region and earned the right to compete at the global level to Shanghai. It was a cohort of the 'best of the best' within Philips and was judged by the senior leadership of Royal Philips, including our CEO, Frans van Houten. The commitment of the senior leadership is essential to the success of a programme such as this and Royal Philips' employees are fortunate that their leadership have maintained this commitment for many years and, in the last few years, have seen a redoubling of the focus.

Why you need a business excellence competition

Although many people may like the idea of a business excellence competition (BEC), one of the challenges that you will have is convincing others, particularly those in the leadership who have to pay for it and sanction the investment of time that team members will make in it. This won't be easy, as the business case is not an easy one to create. However, made it must be and so here are some tips to make it happen:

1. Make approval of, and lobbying for, the business excellence competition a key element of the change and communication strategy.
2. Develop the business case through research of other companies' approaches, understanding clearly the costs and both the tangible and intangible benefits that they derive.
3. Build a wide support base across the business, engaging with senior leaders and influencers across the functions and geography as applicable.
4. Be prepared to start small, either in geography or function, to pilot and showcase the approach.
5. Make replication a core element of the competition and put in place replication targets, with a focus on quality, service, cost and people engagement as the metrics.
6. Determine clear criteria for the competition, which are firmly linked to the strategy of the business, with a theme that resonates with the current focus, for example, zero defects or customer excellence.
7. Gain sponsorship at the highest level possible and make it as much as possible 'theirs'.

Fundamentally, a successful Lean Transformation needs a business excellence competition as a key element of its change management, utilising the Lean Transformation to celebrate success, rewarding and recognising those teams that are pioneering the approach and mindset, while ensuring that the Yokoten[2] learning (knowledge sharing and transfer) is supported. By definition the high-profile parts of the competition may gain the most attention, but the most important element of the business excellence competition is that if forms a continuous process throughout each year and across the years, rather than becoming a distant set of events. This is why it is so important and why we need it as an enabler of our Lean Transformation. It brings together the improvement activities of our team members from across the organisation.

This is not only relevant to large organisations such as Philips but also to smaller, single-site locations, where we can still recognise, reward and replicate our best improvement activity on a more modest scale. Whilst it is true that larger organisations suffer chronically from a lack of communication and knowledge sharing due to geography, functional silos and scale, a team only needs to get beyond a dozen or so people before the barriers of knowledge sharing are erected.

Setting up the business excellence competition

Once the approval has been gained, the real hard work begins, as the Lean Leader and the organising team devise, create and deploy the competition. This requires some thought and it is important that the competition is reflective of the size of the organisation, its history and culture and its vision and mission. While showing respect for the past, it must reflect what the organisation wants to be and therefore needs to embody the future.

I have seen a number of approaches and, although there is no clear right or wrong approach, some of the key elements of a successful business excellence competition are:

1. The competition can begin as a pilot in a part of the business, but it must quickly become a company-wide initiative.
2. It must have top-management sponsorship and engagement, with the leadership, preferably the owner, CEO or managing director and their leadership in attendance and active on the panel of jurors.
3. The process should be continuous, with each year's competition simply a follow-on from the previous one. Continuous improvement initiatives that are entered into the competition are just that, continuous and driven by business need, not the competition.
4. To support this, each cycle of the BEC will start immediately after the final of the last, ensuring that the entrants see clearly that it is an ongoing activity and not an event triggered by a milestone.
5. Replication must feature prominently in the competition, with all entrants expected to promote and execute replication, with follow-up and a prominent award for the best replication.
6. The final must have some element of 'razzmatazz' and ceremony around it, which will be dependent upon the size and culture of the organisation. It must feel like a privilege to be a part of the BEC and highly desirable to all employees.
7. The event must be managed successfully each time and publicised heavily, utilising the change and communication plan.

The Lean Leader will put together an organising committee made up of team members from around the organisation, ensuring that it is representative, and negotiate a budget sufficient to meet the objectives of the competition on the scale agreed. It is very important that the budget limit is respected by the committee and therefore strict management of expenditure is required. The committee will spend time canvassing opinion from across the organisation on expectations and requirements but will also take best practice from external organisations and will realise that the vision for the Lean Transformation means that a large number of the people that they are canvassing will currently be unconsciously incompetent and so they must be careful to listen to the intent of their responses rather than the specifics. It is important that the BEC represents how things will be done in the future and not how they were done in the past.

The organisation of the BEC will need a significant investment of time, regardless of its scale, and an appropriately resourced team will be required. In an organisation of any significant scale it is likely that a full-time lead will be necessary but it is essential that this is not someone who is pulled off the Lean Transformation, as that is simply redeploying resources away from the overall programme. Whilst the person may be part of the business excellence team (see Chapter 14), they have the specific remit to manage the delivery of the BEC. They will coordinate a team of people who are working on the BEC on a part-time basis and so it is important, at a minimum, to have the lead of the competition fully dedicated. Their costs should be a transparent element of the BEC budget, without any of the costs hidden.

The team will meet regularly and follow good project-management practice, establishing a BEC charter, which must be fully agreed by the stakeholders before proceeding and must define the reason for the BEC, its objectives, budget and governance. The objectives will be described with a mix of hard targets around quality, service and cost improvements and soft targets such as employee engagement and Kaizen implementation. Remember that the BEC isn't a discrete event and therefore the objectives will be based on its overall impact on the organisation and not only the impact directly visible in the competition events themselves and will be multiyear, clearly linked to the organisation's Hoshin.

As Lean Thinking will be applied to the BEC and its organisation, a PDCA (plan, do, check, act) approach will be built into the organisation of the competition, ensuring that the project management and metrics are on track and, where not, problem solving is executed. The methodology and activities required to execute the BEC will, naturally, be captured in standardised work, with clear standard operation procedures and work instructions in place in order that the team is able to deploy in a standardised and effective manner, even in a global organisation with multiple locations across geographies. This standardised work will also facilitate the handover and knowledge transfer as team members rotate into and out of the organising team and across the years.

The business excellence competition annual cycle

A typical BEC annual cycle will begin at an appropriate time of the year, which could coincide with the organisation's financial year but is most appropriately designed to facilitate the activist engagement of the senior leadership. The finals should therefore be scheduled at a time of the year when the structured demands on them (such as annual financial reporting to the markets) are at their least.

To illustrate what the cycle would look like, let's take an enterprise that has multiple locations across the Asian, Latin American, North American and EMEA regions. They have set the start and end point of the cycle in June, as this is sufficiently after the end of their financial year (which runs from January to December) and before the summer holiday period to allow for both team members' and senior leadership's involvement in the regional and global finals.

They therefore begin the cycle in June with the launch of the BEC and a message from their CEO. The teams around the world start to prepare their submissions, showcasing their achievements in a standardised format and uploading them onto the BEC data-base, which could be SharePoint or some other global collaboration tool. If this was a very mature organisation, the database would already be populated with these best practices and knowledge sharing as part of the standard practice for all improvement projects and Kaizen events and therefore the teams would simply be deciding upon which of the projects they would enter into the competition.

This process runs for around four months, during which time the locations determine which of their entrants will progress to the market and country finals and prepare the teams for success in those competitions. Some of the locations are a single site, for ex-ample factories of hundreds of team members, whilst other locations are a combination of multiple sites of a few dozen people each. The locations have been set up dependent upon their scale and type of activity, for example, with R&D or sales offices coalesced to provide sufficient scale. Where a market or country has limited activity, such as where there are only sales activities, the local selection and market or country finals are com-bined to create sufficient scale of competition.

Around October to December, the market and country finals take place and the selec-tion of the entrants for the regional finals is made. Even within a market or country, the travel requirements may be high and the budget under pressure, so communication technology and virtual finals are used in many cases. To facilitate this, a standardised ap-proach is taken and short videos created ahead of the finals to allow the jurors to make their selection in as unbiased a manner as possible.

Based on the selection of the market and country finals winners, the regional finals are undertaken in January to March, with a big focus on the involvement of the senior leadership. This means that the most senior leaders in each region, plus some global leaders, are represented on the juries and have made their attendance a high priority. Whilst there will always be some customer-focussed activity that causes one or two of the senior leaders to be unavailable, the majority have planned ahead for the events and only true emergencies get in the way of their attendance.

By the end of March the regional finals are completed and the global finalists confirmed. By June the global finals are in full swing, with the CEO and their leadership team a key part of the jury. Winners are selected for each of the criteria and celebrations are held for these 'best of the best' winners. It is an important moment in the organisation's annual cycle.

The above process can be summarised as follows:

June:	Launch of the BEC annual cycle
June - October:	Local selection
October - December:	Market / country finals
January - March:	Regional finals
June:	Global final

The previous example of a global organisation might risk giving the impression that a BEC is only for a large organisation, but this is not the message that I would want the reader to take from this. Ultimately there should be a final and, in terms of size, I would recommend around 20 teams. This means that most organisations beyond the size of a small family business can run a BEC. The question is really what the scale of it would be. This means that whilst an organisation of 20,000 people might have local selection, country or market, regional and global finals, a single-site enterprise of 100 people might have a single BEC final. The scale itself doesn't matter; what matters is the engagement of all the team members.

Regardless of the scale of the organisation and the number of rounds, one thing that is extremely important is that, at the end of each cycle, there is some form of celebration for the organising team, as they will have been working extremely hard to make it all happen and will probably have been somewhat anonymous, as the participating teams have taken the limelight. It is therefore essential that they are recognised for their great work and thanked for the effort that they have made.

Another consideration for most organisations with a global footprint is the language that will be used in the competition. For the local competition rounds, the local languages can be used but, possibly at the market level, where a market consists of more than one country and certainly at the regional and global level, a lingua franca (common language) will be required. For most global organisations this will be English and for those participants working in global functions or at a certain level in the enterprise, English will be something that they can use without too many problems. In fact their improvement team may consist of multiple language speakers and they may already be working in English on a daily basis. However, for an organisation with a lot of people in more manual and locally focussed roles, particularly where a lot of their team members are in manufacturing or supply-chain and logistics centres, careful consideration must be given to:

1. How the sharing of knowledge is managed to ensure that the improvement efforts of a team in, for example, a factory in China can be shared effectively in a factory in Hungary. This will require the solid use of visual management and a global coding system so that improvements in a certain element of work, for example spot welding, may be found and utilised regardless of location and local language.
2. When it comes to participation in the BEC, it is important to answer the question of how those team members not fluent in the lingua franca can participate. This will mean that some team members of those teams that have made it through to the global finals get some additional language training or that an interpreter is made available. Personally I've seen team members from across the world present at the global finals, when it has been their first time overseas and presenting in English. It is humbling to see the dedication and commitment that they put into doing this. This effort must be reciprocated by the organising committee in ensuring that native-speaker teams do not have an advantage in the scoring over non-native speakers.

The jurors, the awards and the selection criteria

As discussed, there must be senior leadership participation in the BEC and their activism as members of the juries is a fantastic way to secure it. It is important to gain a good cross-section of leadership involvement, with the CEO, managing director or owner and their direct leadership team in at least the global final but as early as possible, and the local and regional leadership involved during the appropriate stages. It is also very important to bring in a good cross-section of functions, to avoid bias toward or against certain functions.

It is amazing to experience the role of being a juror on a BEC panel and everyone who

I've ever spoken to afterwards has commented enthusiastically about how rewarding they found it. It is not unusual for jurors at Philips to have been on multiple juries over the years. It is always difficult for anyone, particularly senior leaders, to invest the time, but the return on that investment is immense in terms of the engagement that they are able to make with the team members and the learning that they gain.

In terms of the awards for the teams, they must be consistent throughout each stage of the competition and the winners of each stage should progress against the same criteria. The awards can be selected by the organisation based upon its own particular strategic and transformation goals but some examples are:

1. Overall winner
2. Replication award (as discussed earlier)
3. Quality (such as zero defects, net promoter score improvement, etc.)
4. Innovation (e.g. best new product, consumer desirability, etc.)
5. Growth (sales revenue increase)

It is important that the awards are meaningful within the organisation and that it is clear that the winners of the awards have had a tangible and measurable positive impact on the business.

In some cases it may be relevant to have awards for each division or sector of a company, although this should only be encouraged where there is a true reason for it, for example if one division is fundamentally less excitingly innovative and therefore its teams might struggle to compete against other divisions which are more cutting-edge in their innovation. Nevertheless, in my experience a choice of separate awards for each division is usually political in nature rather than for good competitive reasons. I would therefore encourage the reader to focus on developing and executing a BEC that is well enough designed, with awards relevant to the total organisation's strategic objectives and a set of selection criteria and a jury system that is beyond reproach so that, in the event of a division winning more than its mathematical share of awards, there can be no doubt that it was well deserved.

In order that the impact is credible and the assessment of all participants fair, clear criteria must be in place that can be applied evenly by all jurors. This is an important role of the organising team and the Lean Leader must ensure that ample thought and preparation is put into setting them and adequate training of the jurors undertaken. To ensure that the application is as even as possible, at least at the global and regional Finals, members of the organising team will provide support in training and aligning the teams and a form of calibration will be applied to ensure that the final decision can be made with confidence.

During each competition event, the participating teams will know what the general criteria are that they will be measured against but will not be provided with the specific scoring criteria, as it is important that they are not enabled to play the competition specifically to the criteria. To avoid this and also to ensure that the specific theme of the organisation that year is supported, it can be useful to modify the scoring criteria on an annual basis, providing an element of mystery for the participating teams and encouraging them to focus purely on their improvement activity, the showcasing of their approach and its business impact.

Inevitably those teams that come from a sales or marketing background will typically be better at pitching during the competition but, to avoid form overshadowing content, the jurors and the organisers should focus on ensuring that they identify clear proof points to support their scoring for each team and that the calibration is as dispassionate as possible in its assessment. Additionally, those teams who have a cross-functional composition overall and in their representation at the competition (in cases where the team was too large for all members to participate) should be rewarded as part of the criteria. This will encourage both cross-functional teamwork in improvement projects and representation at the competition events.

As mentioned earlier, language is also a consideration for the criteria and it is important that the teams are both encouraged to be as visual as possible in their presentations, negating the impact of language, and also that the scoring criteria and juror approach takes the challenges of language into consideration and avoids an unfair advantage for the native speakers. This is not easy of course but it is possible if the right planning is applied, it is considered in the briefing of the jurors and the calibration accounts for it.

Getting teams engaged in the business excellence competition

It is hopefully clear by now that the business excellence competition is central to the engagement of the team members with the Lean Transformation and that its success is measured, ultimately, by the level of that engagement. The vision must be that the team members will continuously share the knowledge created during their continuous improvement activities and that the BEC will simply be a celebration of this. However, to get to that point takes a lot of hard work, so the Lean Leader must ensure that the BEC is highly valued by the team members.

If the BEC is seen only as a management requirement, with participation driven hard by the leadership, it might have a certain appeal and be marketable but it will not resonate with the team members and its potential for business impact will remain unrealised.

However, where instead it is simply an element of the learning organisation that is being created through the Lean Transformation, it will begin to have a deep and meaningful impact on the enterprise.

Fundamental to this is that each BEC interaction is a celebration of the organisation's continuous improvement activity. Where projects and Kaizen events are implemented, the local leadership use the competition to ensure that these efforts are celebrated and that the teams are encouraged and coached into recording and sharing the benefit across the organisation. Equally at the finals, the BEC allows the organising team and the leadership to publicise and celebrate the recognition.

Whilst the recognition of those teams and team members who have made a difference is essential, employees will really engage with the BEC and the learning organisation that it helps to create when two components in place:

1. A knowledge system that benefits them with quick and easy access to best practices and learning, one which makes their job easier to do and improve.
2. A compulsion to participate, through continuous improvement (daily Kaizen), the use and maintenance of standards and the sharing of improvement activity being a requirement of the job.

In essence we need the 'carrot and the stick', whereby the first component is one which provides a clear, tangible benefit to the team members, whilst the second is a compulsion or requirement that the Lean Business System must impose. The checking of adherence will be part of the Leadership Kamishibai (Chapter 9) and is part of the gentle reinforcement of standards and requirements that keeps the Lean Business System intact.

A critical component of the jury criteria, central to the Lean Transformation, is the behaviour that the organisation wishes to see modelled. The BEC is a fantastic platform for celebrating the role models of these behaviours. However, it is generally good practice not to have awards which are specifically for the behaviours themselves but instead embed the modelling of behaviours within the award criteria. By doing so the Lean Leader, the BEC organisers and the leadership can ensure that the teams that win are not only those that made the best business impact (the What) but also achieved it in the best way (the How). This aligns perfectly with Lean Thinking and the way that we want to deploy our Lean Transformation.

ROLE MODEL	False Start	Lean Thinking
HOW? (BEHAVIOUR)		
	Failure	Unsustainable
NON-ROLE MODEL		
	BAD	WHAT? (RESULTS) GOOD

The What and the How of Lean Thinking

The behaviours that the organisation chooses will be those most appropriate to the culture that it is trying to create. Nevertheless, it is essential that they are behaviours that support Lean Thinking and the Lean Management Principles,[3] or similar guidelines, are a great proxy for the behaviours that we would like to see in an organisation.

Again, it may be that the business wants to focus on a subset, which changes from year to year. While a long-term focus on purpose could be common across the years, other aspects might be rotated depending on the view of the focus required in the organisation.

The results of the business excellence competition

It has hopefully become clear in the course of this chapter that a business excellence competition brings a number of advantages to an organisation, both tangible and intangible. However, it is important that we be able to measure both and show the business case for the BEC. This is an important role for the Lean Leader.

The typical metrics are very similar, unsurprisingly, to that of the business itself. We would expect to measure the people, safety, quality, service and cost improvements driven by the BEC, plus the degree of replication delivered. These could look something like the following:

1. **People:** Number of Kaizen implemented per employee (preferably with a hard saving associated with it), employee engagement score, NPS (net promoter score) of the BEC
2. **Safety:** Number of safety Kaizen implemented per employee, safety improvement year on year
3. **Quality:** Quality improvement year on year, with field call rate, fall-off rate or other relevant quality measurement
4. **Service:** Delivery performance, with confirmed line item performance (CLIP), requested line item performance (RLIP) or other relevant measure for industry and relevant service metrics for non-manufacturing parts of the business, for example new product introduction to plan
5. **Cost:** Productivity and inventory improvement measurements should be used as relevant to the business but should focus as much as possible on hard savings, those which really impact the P&L (profit and loss) bottom line or balance sheet.
6. **Replication:** This is probably the most important for the BEC, as it should be a measure of the impact of replication on the first five metrics, measuring how much of the result was driven by replication from one location or area of the business to another.

Where applicable and possible, the above should measure the difference in the metrics between those locations engaged with the BEC and those not, to try to differentiate and demonstrate the impact of the BEC. However, the caveat is that this should not be undertaken if the cost of measurement is too great.

There will always be some degree of debate as to whether the improvements would have happened regardless of the BEC but it is for the Lean Leader to make as strong and compelling a case as possible and for the senior leadership to make a decision and sponsor the business excellence competition on the strength of that business case. This is where the engagement and activism of the leadership in the business excellence competition is so important, as they will witness and feel the less tangible benefits, which should augment the measurable metrics and allow them to make a decision based upon a rounded view. For their part, the Lean Leader will be focussed on ensuring that, in alignment with the overall Lean Transformation, replication becomes a natural part of the team members' work, supporting standardisation and supported by the leadership Kamishibai.

Business excellence is a vision that many organisations strive for and a business excellence competition is central to it, forming a critical success factor in its attainment. Just as at Royal Philips, it can become something that all team members can be proud of and aspire to participate in and to be part of a winning team.

HANSEI

Before moving onto the next chapter, please take a few moments to reflect. When it comes to your own way of working, what are:

1. Your key learning points?

....

....

....

....

2. The changes that you could make?

....

....

....

....

3. Current problems that they would help to solve?

....

....

....

....

PART IV
LEADING EXCELLENCE

14. CREATING THE LEAN ENTERPRISE

Being the doctor, not the shopkeeper

The Lean Leader needs to lead the organisation on its journey to reach operational excellence. This destination will be reached through learning and adopting Lean Thinking and, with the use of the four leadership styles of Activist Leadership, Visible Leadership, Mosquito Leadership and Coaching Leadership, they will model, demonstrate, encourage and coach their colleagues.

This requires that the Lean Leader acts not as a shopkeeper, providing whatever their colleagues may ask for, but as a doctor, first understanding the problem that they need to solve and diagnosing its cause before prescribing a treatment. This is a core element of understanding what the customer values, by not focussing on the solution they say they want but instead on the problem they require a solution for. This is synonymous with the comment of Henry Ford, when he said that:

> *If I'd asked my customers what they wanted, they'd have asked for a faster horse.*

Unfortunately this takes a little longer in the short term than simply providing what has been asked for. It will, however, pay dividends, as acting as the doctor, rather than the shopkeeper, will help the team members get past their state of unconscious incompetence, or not knowing what they don't know, into the learning state of conscious incompetence.

The behaviour required by the Lean Leader and their continuous improvement (CI) team of Lean experts to support this is challenging and is sometimes counter-intuitive for both the Lean expert and the recipient of the behaviour. The recipient has most likely asked for the support of the Lean expert and instead of simply getting what they ask for, they are asked a series of questions and asked to invest time in creating a problem statement and developing an A3 charter. This can be annoying to someone who is already extremely busy and just wants the Lean expert to help them by doing what they have asked.

The Lean expert must therefore have both the courage and the resilience not to fall into the trap of taking the easy option and simply doing what has been asked, as it will be a mistake that will certainly come back to haunt them. Instead, they must maintain 'true north' and act as the guide but how they do it will be the difference between a frustrated colleague and one that, through the process, develops an understanding and appreciation of the benefits of doing things with Lean Thinking.

If you're in a hole, stop digging

Imagine a scenario whereby you employed a builder who you'd heard through recommendation was really good at building swimming pools. On the first day the builder arrives with their team and you inform them that they are required for two weeks and that they should start digging a hole in the back garden. Whilst the builder is rather bemused at the request, you are quite insistent that they should go and dig the hole and so the builder takes his team and does what he's been told. During your research you'd read that digging is a key part of swimming pools and so you want to ensure that the builder is focussed on it.

The builder and their team work tirelessly for a week but, upon your return you're disappointed to find a rather deep, small-diameter hole in the corner of the garden, something that looks nothing like a swimming pool and is located in the wrong place. After heated discussions with the builder, it soon becomes clear that, whilst digging a hole might be essential to swimming pool construction, there are many other elements required to ensure its successful completion. After ironing out this confusion and answering some of the builder's questions about the requirements for size, style, usage and budgets, you are informed that the pool can be constructed in six days and are given a quotation that is within budget. However, you are also given an invoice for the seven days of work that the builder and their team have spent digging the original hole.

Digging the Lean Hole

Whilst the above may seem a little ridiculous, it is analogous with many scenarios that I have experienced where a Lean expert has been requested to support a team or project. It is surprisingly common to find that the requestor's motivation seems to be that they have been told that they need a Lean expert by someone (maybe their boss or a colleague who's had great results with Lean Thinking) or that they've heard that they should do a value stream map or run a Kaizen event before executing the project. It is not unusual in this type of scenario that the Lean expert's services are requested for a fixed period of time and that they are expected to be available to facilitate the application of whichever tool or technique it is that the team may believe necessary.

Inevitably in this situation the team experience a similar disappointment to that of the swimming pool metaphor, with some form of Lean Tool or technique having been applied (a hole having been dug) but the business outcome that they desired (the swimming pool) being far from their sight. This results in frustration for both the team members and the Lean expert and is deleterious to their relationship and to the credibility of the Lean Programme in the organisation.

This often happens because both the requester and the Lean expert have forgotten to start with the Why[1] and instead they have both focussed on each of their versions of the What, resulting in confusion over the How. While all of our team members are accountable for properly defining the Why of an activity, the Lean expert must take a leading role in assuming the responsibility not to simply 'dig holes' where they are asked to but instead ensure that a clear problem statement has been defined in order that the objectives of the activity, project or event can be defined and the charter agreed. This 'A3 thinking' approach is core to Lean Thinking and will ensure that the appropriate intervention and Lean methodology is selected and that the team, including the Lean expert, are fully aligned on why they are doing what they are doing, what they aim to achieve and how they will go about doing so.

Often, taking the time to challenge the request for one's time can be difficult for the Lean expert for a number of reasons, including when hierarchically senior people have made the request, due to the momentum or speed of the associated project or programme, or simply because of the time required in the short term to adequately think about the Why (plan) rather than simply reacting to the request (do). However, ensuring rigour around the planning part of the process always results in a better outcome and so these barriers must be overcome.

Lean Thinking is more than just the application of the toolkit and similarly being a Lean expert is more than simply knowing the Lean Tools. It is therefore essential that the Lean expert acts as a Lean Thinking Coach to the organisation, determining where their time can be best spent and refocussing the welcome requests for their help to maximise the impact. This shouldn't and mustn't be done in a distanced or parochial manner but instead through partnering with the requesters and taking them through the development of their A3 charters.

As the well-worn saying goes, 'When you're in a hole, stop digging.' For the Lean expert, and their colleagues, it is critical that they avoid digging holes where they're not needed.

The centre of excellence

In Chapter 4 I discussed the recruitment of the right types of people into the organisation and the use of consultants, external hires and internal recruitment and development. In order that this cohort of people can make a difference, they need to be formed into a continuous improvement (CI) team of Lean experts that can effectively transform the business.

As also discussed in Chapter 4, we don't want to have too large a group of corporate experts but instead what I call 'distributed expertise' throughout the organisation, whereby there are team members throughout the organisation with the requisite Lean Thinking and skills to enable the transformation. This requires a well organised approach to the setting of the deployment model standards, training curriculum and targets. The best approach to this is to establish a centre of excellence or competency centre. At Philips the CI practice has been established as the foundation of Philips Excellence and is the centre of excellence responsible for all of the CI standards across the company.

This centre of excellence will be relatively small and, even in the largest of corporations, will consist of a team of a few Lean experts, a change and communications manager and a knowledge management lead, with the remaining expertise distributed throughout the organisation. This centre of excellence will still act in a virtual manner such that, even in the example of the large corporation, they would be geographically distributed to support the various regions and locations. For example, in a company headquartered in Europe, four might sit in EMEA, three in APAC, two in NA and one in LatAm. This is, of course, simply for illustrative purposes but the point is that the centre of excellence should never be too far from the Gemba.

The centre of excellence (CoE) must be the beacon for change and will set the following standards for the Lean Transformation of the organisation:

1. The Lean Deployment Model (Chapter 5)
2. The Lean expert standards and their recruitment (Chapters 4 and 16)
3. The Lean Learning Curriculum, training and certification (Chapter 4)
4. The change and communication plan (Chapter 3)

5. The business excellence competition and the knowledge database (Chapter 13)
6. Kaikaku experiences and managing the benchmark database (Chapter 10)

The CoE must never become detached from the business and so it is important that the CoE Team Members have objectives shared with the business. Whilst they do need to have leading indicators, such as the number of certified Lean Practitioners, Lean Stage Progression per site, standard work compliance and so on, they must never be able to claim that they have successfully met their objectives if the business overall has failed to meet its goals.

This is again a strain on the Lean expert, as they will have similar pressures to that of their business colleagues and therefore the temptation to work in a traditional manner. This means that a balance of leading and business metrics, in combination with a critical focus on living the Lean Behaviours is required by the head of the CoE. As the Lean Transformation progresses, these balanced metrics will become more prevalent in the business itself, leading to a reduction in the tension between the Lean experts and their business colleagues.

The CoE must consist of the Lean Thought Leadership for the organisation and, as such, its team members must be both empowered and accountable for living the Lean Paradigms and consistently communicating the Lean Vision. This requires that they have the courage to communicate to the organisation through the various media defined in the communication plan and be willing to openly challenge the status quo of the organisation, even when this might feel uncomfortable. Being part of the centre of excellence and creating the Lean Enterprise has that obligation attached to it.

As the CoE gains its credibility and inherent reputation, the demand for its services will increase significantly and it is therefore important that its team have clear initiatives and objectives linked to the organisation's Hoshin Kanri and that they are confident enough to say no to those requests that are not part of the priorities set. This in itself is a skill and in Chapter 16, I discuss what I've termed the 'intelligent no'.

Coaching upward

To create the Lean Enterprise, the Lean Leader and the CoE need to infect the organisation with Lean Thinking and the best way to effect this is through its leadership, although it isn't necessarily the easiest.

In order to do this, as early as possible in the Lean Transformation, the Lean Leader and their experts must win over a few senior leaders who are enthusiastic and willing to be activist in the Lean Transformation. The aim of this is that, through the coaching of these leaders, the multiplier effect on the organisation will be significant, as they begin to model the desired behaviours within their area of the business and thus encourage their people to follow their lead.

This is an ultimately rewarding experience for the Lean experts. They begin to coach people in their organisation who operate at a higher level than they are used to, so provided that the Lean expert is up to the task, it can become a symbiotic relationship, as both learn from each other and augment their understanding of the business and how to achieve operational excellence.

Nevertheless, this coaching relationship, that of coaching upward, is fraught with difficulty, as the first requirement is for the senior leader to accept the coaching of a junior in the organisation, not necessarily because of an inherent attitude that the subordinate cannot teach them anything but due to their doubts over the Lean expert's understanding of how the business operates at a level of understanding commensurate with theirs. This is the second challenge of the coaching relationship, as the Lean expert must have the confidence and belief in their ability to understand the strategic operations of the business and to be able to apply their Lean expertise to its improvement.

The Lean Leader must therefore ensure that the recruitment of their Lean experts has focussed not only on their Lean Tool and project management skills that are common in the majority of Lean experts but also the less commonly available business acumen and ability to influence at a senior leadership level. They must further spend significant time coaching and developing their Lean experts in order that they discharge their leadership coaching duties adequately and effectively.

Despite the challenges, once the momentum starts to build, a virtuous cycle is created, as word of mouth gets around those leaders not yet involved and the demand for the coaching increases to the point of critical mass. Again, the Lean Leader needs to have a clear plan of coaching for those leaders prioritised for the early stages and must apply the 'intelligent no' in the event of the coaching demand becoming excessive.

However, whilst building the leadership coaching programme they ought to be building the capacity of Lean experts to provide the coaching and, as those senior leaders pioneering in their own Lean Certification reach the path to Lean expert certification, they can be paired up with their peers and act as additional coaching resources.

Building the leadership impact

By definition, a Lean Organisation must have a Lean Leadership and Leading with Lean must become the norm across all of the leadership and at every level of the organisation. The Lean Leader can no longer be you or I, the people tasked with making the Lean

Transformation happen. In fact, whilst we are known as the 'Lean Guy' or a member of the 'Lean Team', we should realise that we are still far from our goal.

The organisation's leadership should be part of the Lean Curriculum and their certification at the appropriate level is a must. Typically all people in leadership roles, from the team leader right through to the CEO should be certified at the Lean advanced level and, just as with the general population, at least 10% of them have to be certified at the Lean expert level. In fact, in my experience it is an area where overdriving on the certification is not wasteful, as those people in leadership positions are able to make a significant impact on the organisation and therefore, as they work through their certification, their Kaizen activity will be highly impactful on the business, their role modelling highly contagious and the legacy that it leaves in their style of leadership substantial.

To get to this level of certification, Lean Leadership Training is required and the centre of excellence must develop one that meets the needs of the Lean Leader to understand both the Lean Methodology as well as the change and Lean Leadership aspects. This is not an easy course to develop and at Royal Philips it took some time to get right but resulted in training that is highly effective. One of the difficulties of this type of training is that, to truly engross the participant in the softer aspects of Lean Thinking, a substantial contiguous period of time is required. Unlike training in the tools, which can be done in small blocks of say one or two days, to train people in Lean Leadership requires several consecutive days, during which the participant is intensively trained.

In the End2End Lean Leadership Training that we developed at Royal Philips, the participant undergoes eight days of training across two weeks, normally with a weekend in between. The training is delivered by two Lean masters and is fully residential, ensuring that the cohort of between 24 and 32 participants are fully immersed in the learning experience. During the first week, normally running from Tuesday to Friday, the participants are placed in teams of six to eight people, assigned a team colour of red, green, blue or yellow and asked to create their own team image. The teams are concurrently trained in aspects of Lean Leadership and assigned tasks, with the trainers placing the teams in competition with each other, awarding or deducting points from each team on the basis of performance and Lean behaviour adherence. During this first week, the majority of team members, and hence the teams, perform in a traditional manner and hence are unable to adequately deliver the required results or behave in a Lean manner.

During the first week the trainers have taken a traditional approach to their management of the training course and, as such, the participants have mainly been given instruction as to the requirements and penalised when the performance hasn't been met. However, in the second week the trainers take a different approach, whereby they act as coaches to the teams and help them to reflect on their performance, understanding why they aren't performing, setting targets to improve and, through Hansei (deep reflection) developing their Lean behaviours. This allows the teams and their participants to bring themselves through the change curve that they have been experiencing and become high-performance teams and team members. By the end of the second week, whilst one team is always pronounced the competition winner, all of the teams have won in terms of their learning and the performance that they end with.

The training, whilst intense, is only the first part of these potential Lean Leaders' learning process, as coming out of the training they are assigned a personal Lean Coach and must complete a 30-60-90-day follow-up plan, which if successfully executed results in their certification at the Lean advanced level of certification, the equivalent of a green belt level of certification. While the naming of the follow-up plan implies that the improvement project or Kaizen Event that they undertake takes 90 days, this is only the expected minimum duration of the plan and do elements of the PDCA cycle, as the check and act phases would normally take longer, with the typical duration to completion being around 6-9 months. However, once certified, this is the platform for the continuation to Lean expert and, ultimately, Lean master level and many of the graduates continue their Lean Leadership learning journey.

Although not every organisation will choose or need such an intensive approach to the development of their Lean Leaders, it is my experience that those truly Lean-Thinking organisations have, one way or another, taken their Leadership through a significant amount of Lean Leadership training, coaching and development and the reader should think seriously about how they will make this happen in their organisation.

Enterprise-wide transformation

This chapter is entitled 'Creating the Lean Enterprise' and, throughout, the focus has been on the leadership aspects and their development, as they are essentially the difference between the Lean Enterprise and the rest. The Lean Transformation Model that you use will, whether it is the VIRAL model or another, have a replication stage where the learning from the model value streams and sites is scaled across the whole organisation. The inherent risk in this is that it becomes a technical rollout, whereby the tools and methodology are scaled but the leadership and Lean behaviours aren't.

However, the enterprise-wide transformation can and will only happen when the leadership approach is scaled and so the training, coaching and certification of our leaders must be front and centre in the transformation approach and once again the centre of excellence plays a key role in this, undertaking 'Kamishibai' on the organisation to ensure that shortcuts aren't being taken in replicating the successes of the model stage.

HANSEI

Before moving onto the next chapter, please take a few moments to reflect. When it comes to your own way of working, what are:

1. Your key learning points?

2. The changes that you could make?

3. Current problems that they would help to solve?

15. BREAKING THE MEDIOCRITY BARRIER

The definition of mediocrity

In the Oxford English Dictionary, the definition of mediocrity is given as:

1. The state of being mediocre
2. A person of mediocre ability

Given this definition, I'm pretty certain that mediocrity is not something that any organisation or individual would ever admit to exhibiting or aspiring to. Nevertheless, it is one of the biggest barriers to delivering change in an organisation.

Consider Kotter's eight-step change management model, where one of the biggest issues is that the first step, creating a sense of urgency, is often difficult unless an organisation is truly in crisis. For most organisations, whilst its senior leaders, investors and the majority of employees might accept that the performance is not at the desired level to ultimately prosper, they generally don't have a sufficient sense of a 'burning platform' to commit to the change for themselves.

Change is for everyone else

Therefore, for large parts of the organisation change is seen as something that others need to make, as they consider their own performance as adequate and easily improvable if only others would act differently and, while they may use the right language, their actions clearly demonstrate that the transformation will not be successful.

This can be quite frustrating for those people tasked with the role of business transformation and is accentuated if the approach taken for change is focussed on telling people What they need to do instead of ensuring that the Why and How have first been clearly internalised by the majority of the team members. Simon Sinek codified the 'Start with Why' approach to success extremely well and the TED Talk on this subject is well worth the time.

Where the organisation is able to gain enough momentum to gain some traction, the mediocrity barrier often ultimately results in its failure at Step 7 of Kotter's model, which states, 'Don't let up'. The 'quick wins' attained in Step 6 create a false sense of achievement and result in the declaration of victory too soon, meaning that management attention and the 'guiding coalition' of Step 2, which have helped to foster the success to date, dis-integrate and the focus is moved back onto day-to-day activities. This leaves the change managers in a lonely position and results in degradation of results over time.

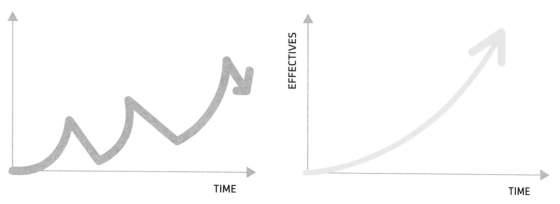

Inconsistent vs. consistent change activity

So how can an organisation ensure that it breaks through the mediocrity barrier? Well, it should be no surprise by this stage in the book that leadership is a key element of this and that a sustained, people-focussed approach is required. The change process must be managed using a structured and proven approach, such as Kotter's eight-step model, and change leadership is absolutely essential.

A powerful technique for assessing whether the change leadership is in place is the VCRSP test, which is an initialism for 'vision, commitment, resources, skills and plan', and is an excellent way to establish whether the right conditions are in place, both at the beginning of the transformation and throughout the process. Where evidence arises that one or more of the VCRSP tests are failed, the leadership must take action or risk the (almost certain) deterioration of effectiveness of the change.

The burning platform

In Chapter 5 the subject of change enablers was raised and the initials that act as their mnemonic, VCRSP, were introduced. The importance of these change enablers to the Lean Transformation, and to avoiding mediocrity, cannot be over-emphasised, so it's important to cover them in a bit more detail in this chapter.

Vision: In order to set the vision for the organisation, the leadership must first have iden-tified the 'burning platform' for change and fully established the Why for communication, with a clear articulation of where the organisation is headed. This must be in terms of both improvement in business performance and what it will mean for the employees and other stakeholders. The vision must be customer-centric and people-focussed and engage the employees in a motivating vision of the future.

Some thought leaders in the field of change have a certain allergy to the term 'burning platform' and I can understand this, as it is possible that it could be perceived as too extreme a term or that it might incite negative connotations in the minds of our colleagues. In fact, I recently heard an excellent and inspiring thinker in operational excellence, speaking at a conference in London, where he said something along the lines of:

> **If I was on a Burning Platform I might be inclined to help put out the fire but I would certainly ensure that my exit was clear and be ready to exit when it was needed.**

I understand the thinking behind this, that the metaphor could be perceived as saying that the organisation is in big trouble and that we need to put out a large fire, which might scare off, rather than motivate, some of our staff.

However, I don't believe that this is the true meaning of the metaphor, as the etymology appears to be the story of the Piper Alpha Oil Rig and specifically one of its inhabitants and workers, Andy Mochan, who, on that disastrous evening in July 1988, chose possible death over certain death and jumped from the burning rig into the freezing cold waters of the North Sea. The metaphor is therefore not intended to imply that we have a large fire that needs to be put out but rather that the cost of sustaining the status quo (staying on the platform) is higher than the cost of making the change (jumping into the freezing cold sea).

These are the critical elements of the vision, that the employees and stakeholders of the organisation must understand why the change is necessary and what is in it for them. Otherwise, without a compelling Why, many of them will say, 'Why change? It's not that bad.' Of course, the reality of an organisation's reason for change will never involve the seriousness of a human disaster such as the Piper Alpha and those of us who use this metaphor do not do so with any lack of respect for those whose lives have been affected by such disasters. Nevertheless, as with most metaphors, there is an element of exaggeration that is intended to emphasise the seriousness of the subject. It is therefore essential that the leadership, supported by the Lean Leader, establish the 'burning platform', 'case for change', 'reason for revolution' or whichever term resonates best with the organisation's people.

The difficulty of this will depend upon the organisation's situation and the degree of synchronicity between the organisation and its people's interests. To explain, in the first case the immediacy of the problems of the organisation will have a bearing on the ease of making the case for change. For example, if the company is on the edge of bankruptcy, the case for change will be relatively easy to make, whereas if the company is highly profitable and a market leader, it would be a much more difficult case to prove that it needs to make the metaphorical jump. In that case the leadership would need to determine the long-term implications of not changing and create an immediacy that can be easily communicated to the workforce.

In the case of the synchronicity of the organisation and its people's interests, there are a number of organisations where even when they might be in extremely difficult times, their people do not recognise the direct link between its successful future and theirs. This can be for a number of reasons but commonly this is found in the public or highly unionised sectors, where the relative, some might say artificial, employment security is a buffer against any sense of urgency for change. For the Lean Leader and the organisation's leadership, this can make it even more difficult to create the 'burning platform' but is a requisite of a successful transformation.

The chicken and the pig

The second element of the VCRSP test of change is commitment, which starts and must be sustained by the leadership.

Commitment: In order that the transformation not only starts but is sustained, commitment is required throughout and at every level of leadership. As was discussed in Chapter 7, in the metaphor of the chicken and the pig, commitment requires not only advocacy for the Lean Deployment but also activism to be a part of the change. Above all, it's the senior leadership that must be fully committed to the change and be willing to accept that they will have to change as much as, if not more than, the rest of the employees. The change starts with them and will then cascade throughout the organisation as priorities and expectations are aligned across the business. The behaviours that got them where they are today are not those that will get them where they want the organisation to go to and so they need to be role models in the change. This means Leading with Lean with the four leadership styles and ensuring that communication is clear, consistent and frequent.

They will have to show, through action, that mediocrity will not be tolerated, that excellence is expected, and be willing to support those in their teams who begin to live and breathe the principle. A quality mindset will and must become the rule and not the exception, not only in the end product or service but in every element of the value chain. All too often quality is perceived as an end product and something to be measured at the point of readiness for the customer, whereas true quality is in everything that we do, whether it is in the process for determining the customer value proposition, the design of the product or service, the invoicing to customers or purchase orders to suppliers. Essentially it is about believing that everything we do must be done right the first time, with the minimum of activities that the customer doesn't value. This is Lean Thinking and the space in which mediocrity ceases to be.

The engagement of all employees must be managed effectively and, again, clear communication around the vision and what employees should expect is crucial. Linking to the vision, honesty is mandatory for success and, whilst the avoidance of job losses or redundancies directly related to the Lean Transformation should always be the objective, if the vision includes an organisation that in the short term remains similar in size but, due to the removal of waste will require fewer people, this ought to be part of the honest communication with the employees. Honesty and integrity in the communication of the vision are the most important elements in gaining the commitment of the people and should not be underestimated.

Where redundancies are a possible consequence of the transformation, it can be challenging for the leadership and to do this, they must truly believe in two things related to their vision:

1. The cost of not transforming (maintaining the status quo) is greater than that of the change, which includes the potential loss of jobs.
2. That the transformation will make the organisation fitter, more agile and better placed for the future, ultimately leading to growth and job creation.

The change required to transform the business requires commitment but, above all, as will be covered in Chapter 20, stamina is the main differentiator between those organisations that are successful and those that are not. Unfortunately, it is often the senior leaders who give in first.

Resources: In order for the transformation to be effective, resources will need to be made available, including people (both internal and external), finance and time. The organisation will need to invest in people to facilitate, guide and coach the organisation throughout the process. The investment in these resources will be part of the leadership commitment and finance will be required for external resources where specific competencies or skills are required and for changes that might be made to layouts or set-ups as part of the Lean Transformation. In Lean Thinking, the idea is not to invest in expensive automation or capital-intensive solutions and so the financial investment should be modest in comparison to typical transformation, new product introduction or IT projects. However, linking back to the commitment aspect, time will be something that the leadership will need to invest and is probably the most important resource that they can provide as Lean Leaders.

The investment in people is important and links back to the vision, which requires that people with the right mindset and understanding of the strategy are in the right positions. However, it must also be realised that employee turnover may be affected in times of change and therefore efforts must be redoubled in terms of succession planning for key positions and the development of multiskilling. As the transformation of the business becomes more mature, it is natural that some of the key drivers of change will be recruited by other organisations and this must be managed and also accepted as a collateral part of success, rather than failure.

Change is a double-edged sword in terms of resources as it provides opportunities for some and inspires fear in others. Generally, those employees earlier in their career, lower in the organisation's hierarchy or perhaps with less personal financial commitments will see the change and the new openings as the chance to take a risk and perhaps gain a promotion or new aspects to their CV that will make them more attractive as candidates for more senior or interesting roles either inside or outside the organisation.

By contrast, those employees with a longer tenure, more seniority or larger personal financial commitments might find the changes intimidating and be more resistant to becoming involved. Ignoring this and focussing only on those employees who are most enthusiastic can be a mistake, as it risks missing out on the expertise and skills of a large cohort of team members who, with a little encouragement and coaching, could bring much to the transformation.

Skills: A common error in a transformation or any change programme is to neglect the skills of the people. This includes not only the change agents, such as the Lean experts, who will, of course, need to be adequately skilled to undertake the task, but all employees. Often high-performing employees are assumed to be able to undertake the task with their current competence. This is a big mistake, as high performers often start to fail during times of change due to a lack of Lean change management, project management and soft skills. It is therefore very important to ensure that a mix of experienced Transformation Leaders, combined with high-performance individuals who are given the right training and coaching, are recruited into the roles. Allied to this, the range of competencies required for all employees in the Transformed organisation must be identified and developed throughout the process.

The leadership styles presented in *Leading with Lean* are applicable at every level of the organisation and will need to be taught to supervisors, managers, directors and 'C-level' executives. However, the challenges will be different at each level, with a particular challenge at the middle level of the organisation.

The management sandwich

The middle level of management are, in my experience, the most challenging cohort of leaders to break through from traditional thinking to lean thinking. To illustrate this, think about your Lean Deployment and Transformation activity as a sandwich - whichever you prefer, be it tuna mayo, cheese and ham or BLT. Now think about the bottom piece of bread as the team members, the filling as the middle management layer(s) and the top piece of bread as the top management. There you have your management sandwich.

In this management sandwich, when we apply Lean Thinking we quickly stimulate our pieces of bread, with the team members getting the opportunity to use their ideas and to team up with their colleagues to improve the business performance. While there may be some organisations that use Lean as a short-term headcount reduction exercise, yours is one that is looking long-term and is aiming to do more with the same. The team members see the opportunities that this creates for them.

The top management also see the benefits, as customer service levels increase, the business starts to grow and the operational metrics improve significantly. They've made the right choice to go with a Lean Transformation of their business and are experiencing Lean in much the way that Art Byrne talked about in *The Lean Turnaround*.[1]

However, the filling isn't doing as well out of this. They're seeing their staff becoming autonomous, they're not asked to solve every problem anymore, as their team members are rapidly solving problems and they are expected to act as coaches. They must work with Leader Standard Work and are asked to undertake strange Lean Management activities, such as Kamishibai, whilst at the same time the kudos and credit goes to their bosses, whose idea this was. All in all, their reality and paradigms are changing rapidly and they're not feeling too well. The change curve is in full throttle: fasten your seatbelts! It is therefore extremely important that the middle level of leadership are provided with the support that they need to make the change, as they are critical to the success of the transformation and their leadership skills therefore need to be a key focus. This will require some pretty heavy-duty training and development and you will find that those companies most successful in their Lean Transformations have invested heavily in the development of this level of leadership.

My advice is to invest in a Lean Leadership Certification Programme, which fulfils the leadership requirements. It is important to emphasise the certification element of the programme, as opposed to simply training. This will, of course, require training but the participants will also be expected to continue to demonstrate the application of their learning through a Kaizen project that makes a modest but impactful change to their area and involves them training, coaching and developing their team members.

An example of this is the training programme developed at Philips and discussed in Chapter 14, named End2End Lean Leadership, which takes the participants through eight days of intensive training across two weeks. During the training, which is organised as a team competition, the participants are trained and coached in Lean Thinking and work through an accelerated change curve, as they experience the positive impact on performance of moving from traditional to Lean Thinking.

At the start of the training they form teams and are provided with tasks that are extremely challenging, putting them under a high degree of pressure. Inevitably they neglect to consider their team formation process or the Lean way of approaching problem solving, instead falling into traditional firefighting approaches which result in low quality, late delivery and high cost in terms of their working extended hours. However, as the teams are coached through the training, they begin to adopt Lean ways of working, developing better team dynamics and improved performance, which reinforces the learning modules presented throughout the training. At the end of the training course they take a written exam to test their learning, which aims not to catch any of the participants out but simply to reinforce the learning. After the course they must complete their Lean Project to achieve certification.

In Chapter 4 I shared the different levels of expertise development, from Foundational through to master level. We would expect all of our leaders to become certified at the advanced level as a minimum and a significant minority to achieve Lean expert certification, modelling Lean Leadership to their peers and team members.

Planning for success

To recap the chapter, so far we've covered the vision, commitment, resources and skills that are required to drive change and break the mediocrity barrier. However, to make all of this work, there is a final element that is required.

Plan: To make it all work a solid plan must be in place that contains all of the attributes of the transformation. The plan will not be a static document and will never survive the 'first shot of battle', so it is essential that robust project management is applied throughout the transformation and the leadership must be agile as it adapts to bumps in the road while maintaining the true north of the vision.

The plan is essential, as without one we will suffer from scope creep, as the early successes will drive demand for the services of the Lean experts and transformation managers and we will risk spreading our resources too thinly. As will be discussed in Chapter 16, the Lean Leader must apply the 'intelligent no' if they are to ensure that their resources are adequately focussed and the plan is a great defence against this. Without a plan there is also the risk of misalignment amongst the leadership, as initial agreements mean nothing without the discipline that a written plan instils and, as discussed in Chapter 6, Hoshin Kanri should have been instilled in the organisation if the vision is to be honoured.

The Lean Leader is the steward of the plan, which is derived from the vision that has been set, demanding the leadership demonstrate their commitment through it. The plan must be holistic and includes the resources and skills development as well as the communication plan.

The VCRSP test is a critical but often neglected part of change management. Through the disciplined execution of the process, true change leadership can be practised and the organisational transformation navigated. When this is done, the Lean Leader can help the enterprise through the mediocrity barrier and toward true excellence.

VISION		COMMITMENT		RESOURCES		SKILLS		PLAN	
V	x	C	x	R	x	S	x	P	= Change
?	x	C	x	R	x	S	x	P	= Confusion
V	x	?	x	R	x	S	x	P	= Rejection
V	x	C	x	?	x	S	x	P	= Frustration
V	x	C	x	R	x	?	x	P	= Anxiety
V	x	C	x	R	x	S	x	?	= False start

The VCRSP test

HANSEI

Before moving onto the next chapter, please take a few moments to reflect. When it comes to your own way of working, what are:

1. Your key learning points?

2. The changes that you could make?

3. Current problems that they would help to solve?

16. MAKING THE BUSINESS EXCELLENCE TEAM EXCELLENT

Recruiting the right people

The Lean Enterprise needs coaches who know what excellence looks like. The challenge is finding those people who are willing to step away from the operational activity to coach and teach others in business excellence and what often happens is that those less able to perform in the operational arena are placed in a business excellence role or that certain people make it a career in itself without ever having spent significant time in an operational role.

However, with perhaps a few notable exceptions, an approach to resourcing a team to support the Lean Transformation that in the main relies on team members without significant operational experience and high performance will be doomed to failure. It is therefore imperative that the Lean Leader identifies and recruits those people in the organisation who are the most desirable candidates for the operational roles and that the organisation supports this. In essence, the philosophy behind this approach is that an excellent performer, with significant experience, can have a multiplier effect on the business beyond that which they could have in an operational role.

This approach to recruitment is difficult and is a challenge to the normal sensibilities of the organisation, which will struggle with the usual difficulties of finding talent for their operational roles. To then ask a manager to sacrifice one of their best performers to the Lean Team is counterintuitive to normal human behaviour and must be managed by the senior leadership in terms of making the decision non-negotiable but at the same time rewarding the manager losing the person with something of value, such as first refusal on the next talent.

Another barrier to this recruitment approach is that the potential candidates will not see the benefit of stepping out of their well-defined career paths and into the unknown. This is a natural reaction and completely understandable but it is essential that this barrier is removed and this requires that the leadership commit to, and follow through on, fast-track promotions for those people who take on these roles and perform.

This will normally require their commitment for a three-year assignment but in return they will move into a role, pending performance, that is at least one grade above their current level and with a well-defined career path for further development. By doing this the organisation balances out the risk-reward equation of stepping outside of the standard career path for a team member.

The investment by an organisation's leadership in the talent that it places in the Lean Transformation roles is a critical success factor in terms of both the message that it sends to the rest of the organisation and the high impact created by the talent that it places in these positions.

Enabler = accountable

To be successful, the business excellence team must be enablers of business excellence in the organisation and must not take the short-term approach of doing the work for the team members. This is the difference described in the metaphor between giving someone a fish for the day or teaching them to fish; the business excellence team member, let's say a Lean champion, must metaphorically teach them to fish.

However, this does not mean that the Lean champion is not responsible for the business results and can excuse their own performance by saying that they did everything that they could. Ultimately, if the pupil hasn't learnt, then the teacher hasn't taught and so if the business didn't reach its targets, then the Lean champion must take responsibility for that underperformance.

What this means is that the Lean champion must ensure that they are fully aligned to the Why and What of the organisation and their challenges, coaching and training of the team members and their leadership must be based upon the How, which should and must deliver better results than the traditional approach. This will require the full support of the business excellence leader / Lean master, who will need to ensure that the approach being prosecuted by their team members is supported by the leadership and therefore tenable.

The business excellence leader will also have the obligation to ensure that their team's objectives are fully aligned with those of the teams they are entrusted with supporting.

The intelligent no

Saying no is generally considered to be negative and of course, by definition, it is. Therefore saying no is hard to do and most people find it particularly difficult as they develop a reputation for success, or are identified within the organisation as someone who gets things done. Whatever the reason, the demand for their services will inevitably begin to outstrip their ability to meet it and they will therefore face the dilemma of having more demand than capacity.

At this point they have two choices:

1. Overpromise compared with what can be delivered.
2. Say no to the request.

Unfortunately, the majority of people tend to favour Choice 1 for a number of reasons but primarily due to two root causes; firstly the social and hierarchal pressure not to say no and secondly due to the common underestimation of the amount of work involved in their current workload and hence a false belief of having free capacity. The result of this is that they often fail to deliver what they have committed to on time or to the right level of quality, with a number of consequences, including overload for themselves and their colleagues, damaged reputation and strained relationships.

A theme in this book has been the leadership's responsibility to prioritise[1] and the techniques to manage priorities and capacity. While it is incumbent upon the leadership to become better at prioritisation and remaining focussed, it is critical that all employees become adept at understanding their priorities, true capacity and, most importantly, saying no.

However, there is a distinct difference between saying a stark no and in responding with what I refer to as the 'intelligent no', with the fundamental difference being that in the case of the former, the conversation is closed and the requester is dissatisfied with the response, whereas in the latter case, if done well, the requester understands the reason for the no and is happy with the alternative offered.

To illustrate, when beginning a Lean Transformation in an organisation, the business excellence team will inevitably start on a small scale and will (hopefully) experience success. This success will elicit requests from other parts of the organisation and the natural response is to attempt to meet all of the requests. However, if that approach is taken, it is inevitable that the team will fail in some areas, as the demand will simply outstrip their capacity to meet it.

As an alternative, if the team applies the mindset of the 'intelligent no', they will have determined the scope and objectives of Lean deployment and the Lean Leader will have agreed this with the organisation's leadership. These priority areas - let's call them the model lines, will be where the team is expected to focus its efforts. A certain amount of support for all areas of the business will be provided in terms of basic lean foundational training, daily management and problem solving, but the bulk of the capacity will be dedicated to the model lines.

The business excellence team are therefore empowered to say no to other requests, quoting the committed scope of the Lean Transformation, and can have an open and honest dialogue with the requestors, preferably providing them with some advice on how to better utilise the available support or managing their expectations. This apparent lack of support may appear counterintuitive but will be one of the key enablers of success, ensuring that the business excellence resources are focussed on their goals and have sufficient capacity to meet them.

Whilst this example was about a business excellence team, it could equally have been about a new product development team, marketing group, project team or manufacturing cell. Fundamentally, it is about understanding what the priorities are, resourcing those priorities appropriately and then staying focussed on delivering on commitments, without distraction. This is what operationally excellent, world-class organisations do every day and the business excellence team must model and drive this behaviour, utilising Hoshin Kanri and daily management as the key tools of focus.

This does not mean that the teams aren't challenged to do more. They must, of course, get better and reduce the waste in their processes to improve their capacity and performance. They should also not be allowed to 'sandbag' capacity and so the 'intelligent no' doesn't mean that teams are without stretch objectives or high-performance targets. The 'intelligent no' is a call to action for leaders to clearly identify their expectations for their team members, through solid Hoshin Kanri and daily management, Crucially, employees must also ensure that they are accountable for delivery by clearly and honestly utilising the 'intelligent no' to ensure high performance through refusal.

Healthy reporting line tension and a small central team

While the business excellence team must be jointly responsible for the results of the business, the reporting lines of its team members must be independent of the business until the top level. This will ensure that the business excellence team members are able to focus on the How as they see it without being overtly influenced by the business leadership. This natural tension between the business and the business excellence team is essential to ensure that the longer-term transformation goals are not subjugated by the short-term drivers of the business.

At the same time, the business excellence team must not be distinct from the business, or perceived as such, so the team must be embedded in the business on an operational basis. Only a small central team should be in place, responsible for setting the standards for the Lean Transformation and business excellence and acting as a centre of excellence. An effective approach to this is dependent upon the size of the organisation but the 'rule of 10' is a good general approach, whereby we would expect that for every 10 people in the organisation, we would have one of the operational team members certified at the Lean advanced or Six Sigma green belt Level and able to support their fellow team members. At this level, they would be operational and only an associate member of the business excellence team and would report within the operational team structure. However, for every 10 Lean advanced / green belt certified team members (i.e. every 100 people) we would have a Lean expert / black belt certified business excellence team member, who would be fully dedicated to business excellence and reporting through to the business excellence lead.

Further we would have one Lean master / master black belt for every 10 Lean experts and therefore, in an organisation of 10,000 people, we would expect to have around 110 people, or just over 1% of the population, dedicated to business excellence. These people would have a direct reporting structure with the business excellence team but share the business objectives of the groups that they support.

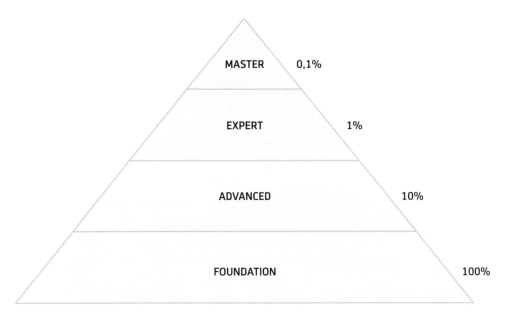

The Lean Certification levels and ratios

The centre of excellence

It is tempting to staff the centre of excellence with career HQ staff but, as discussed earlier in this chapter, it is essential that the staff are actually experienced and high-performing team members. They should be focussed on delivering results through a 'multiplier' effect and therefore should understand extremely well how the business works and how things operate at the shop-floor level.

The centre of excellence (Chapter 14) must be a practically based organisation and, even in a business of 50,000 employees, would not number more than a handful of people. Their tasks are to:

- Develop and maintain the Lean Transformation Model (e.g. The VIRAL model).
- Set the standards for the core activities of Hoshin Kanri, daily management and problem solving.
- Undertake Kamishibai on the businesses and the business excellence team processes throughout the organisation.
- Undertake Kaikaku visits and adopt best practices as applicable.
- Lead the overall change and communication activities for the organisation.
- Lead the best-practice sharing and replication across the enterprise.

The staff in the centre of excellence should be recognised as thought leaders within the organisation and would, as the Lean Transformation progresses, become recognised externally as thought leaders. This, of course, brings with it a retention risk but also helps to develop the reputation of the organisation and acts as a support for recruitment of external candidates.

The profile of the centre of excellence staff will not be easy to fulfil, as they will require a mix of seasoned professional, risk taker, explorer and continuous learner while also being highly motivated. They will be few and far between and, for multi-location organisations, rather than attempt to bring them all to the HQ location, a virtual team should be supported. In the case of multi-location organisations, it is preferable to have this team located geographically in line with the major locations of the business.

The business excellence competition

In Chapter 13 I discussed the important role of the business excellence competition to the Lean Transformation and gave the example of the Philips Excellence Competition, the way in which this drives the celebration, and hence motivation, of our teams to continuously improve and how it contributes significantly to the replication of improvement ideas across the organisation.

I cannot emphasise enough the importance of the business excellence competition in achieving excellence. The role that it plays in coalescing the Global Lean Transformation activities is essential and the focus that it provides is complementary to the efforts of the business excellence resources across the enterprise.

However, whilst the Philips Excellence Competition might be a large-scale, corporate initiative, its essence and philosophy is applicable no matter what the size of the organisation or constituent part might be and the Lean Leader and business excellence organisation must ensure investment in this central aspect of business excellence.

HANSEI

Before moving onto the next chapter, please take a few moments to reflect.
When it comes to your own way of working, what are:

1. Your key learning points?

....

....

....

....

2. The changes that you could make?

....

....

....

....

3. Current problems that they would help to solve?

....

....

....

....

17. RECONCILING THE VALUE STREAM WITH LOCAL AUTONOMY

End-to-end thinking

The Lean Leader is, by definition, an ambitious person and one who wants to make a significant difference to their organisation through their stewardship of its Lean Transformation. Lean Thinking, of course, dictates that we must follow the five elements codified by Womack and Jones:[1]

1. Determine value in the eyes of the customer.
2. Visualise the value stream and remove the waste.
3. Create flow.
4. So that the customer can pull the value.
5. Continuously strive for perfection.

It therefore stands to reason that the Lean Leader must focus on improving the value stream from one end to the other (end-to-end), from the customer all the way back to the creation of the product or service. If they can remove substantial waste in the value stream, they will make a significant improvement in business performance. This is, of course, true and it is absolutely essential that the organisation determines how to transform its value streams comprehensively.

However, as discussed in previous chapters, one of the pitfalls of a traditional, non-Lean, organisation is that only a small cadre of 'experts' solve problems and if the organisation's Lean Transformation is focussed only on the end-to-end transformation of its value streams, this error will be perpetuated. Instead, the Lean Leader must ensure that a balance is achieved between the overall value-stream improvements and the localised continuous-improvement activities that are required to become a Lean Organisation.

The horizontals and the verticals

The horizontals and the verticals refer to the interaction between the value streams and the functions / people who are adding the value throughout the value stream. When managing the Lean Transformation, the Lean Leader needs to ensure that they do not neglect either of these elements. Although improving them on their own can improve business performance, neither on their own will have the transformational effect that we desire.

The Lean Transformation must therefore be planned out and executed to make the change at both levels, which means that in the horizontals, the value streams, the current state, end to end, will be mapped and the current-to–future-state plan created. In terms of the verticals, each function and location of the business will eventually be transformed from traditional thinking and its leadership to Lean Thinkers. These are, of course, not completely separate activities, as the value stream transformation happens in the locations and functions, while the transformation in the locations and functions affects the value stream. Nevertheless, if the Lean Leader only focuses on one element, the overall transformation will suffer.

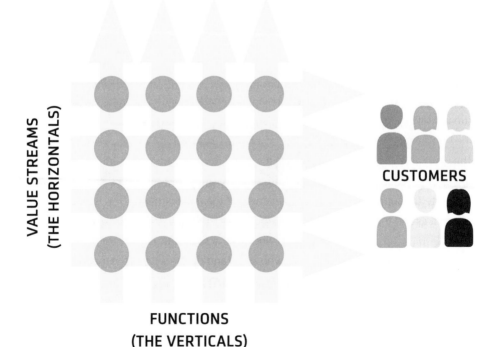

The horizontals and the verticals

The horizontals

For most organisations, regardless of size, their value streams will be complicated and much time will need to be invested to truly understand what their customer values and to map the value stream from the customer all the way back to the creation of the product or service. I am not going to attempt to describe the technical approach for this, as this is not the intention of this book and many others have done this already, probably better than I could.

Nevertheless, as challenging as it might be to map out and understand the whole value stream and to create the future-state vision, it is crucial that it is done for three reasons:

1. Understanding the whole allows the leadership to make fact-based decisions about the future vision.
2. The end-to-end value stream map can only be created when the different functions and people involved in the process are brought together.
3. Functionalisation creates the illusion of value added in every part of the value stream, which must be removed.

Taking the time to build the end-to-end value stream will empower the people who do the work and provide them with the opportunity to demonstrate how the value is provided for the customer, while also locating the waste that gets in their way. The leadership can then support the design of the future state vision and the plan to deliver it over the coming years. Thorough prioritisation will ensure that the transformation planning will be soundly based upon a strong coalition of agreement on which areas of the value stream will be improved and when. This enables the solid planning discussed earlier in the book and supports the VCRSP test covered in Chapter 15.

The Hoshin Kanri planning will devolve the elements of the improvement into the organisational levels and functions and subsequent value-stream maps at those levels will be created to support each particular element of the transformation. This is where the horizontals and the verticals interact, as the improvements in the value streams are only possible in the functions and locations where the activities are carried out. This is why it is so important to involve the people who know and do the work in the mapping and definition of the value stream at the appropriate level.

The verticals

The functions and locations where the work is done will be where the Lean Leader really engages the people and this is often an area where traditional programmes are executed badly. The people involved are often not considered while a new IT tool or process is implemented, with little or no proper consideration of the team members who need to use the new tools or processes.

To transform the organisation it is necessary to improve the overall capability and this requires that the three elements of capability are developed:

1. People competencies and engagement
2. Tools (IT, robotics, automation)
3. Processes

Unfortunately, in the majority of traditional programmes the tools are the main focus, with some attention to the processes, while the people competencies, and their engagement, are largely neglected. There is an almost blind faith that putting in place the best-in-class or latest technological solution will suddenly propel the enterprise to success or that designing the 'perfect' processes in headquarters and imposing them on the staff will result in operational excellence. They won't.Whatever the processes or tools that we implement may be, they are ultimately used, managed and operated by people, so the development of their competencies and engagement is critical to operational excellence. This can seem like it takes more time. As well as project managing the deployment of tools or new processes, we must also ensure that we apply rigorous change management to ensure that our people are engaged in the change and that the requisite competency development is undertaken.

This is not to dismiss the importance of utilising technology and automation to improve the efficiency of processes, but it is only when we ensure that the people element is properly considered that we will achieve true effectiveness. In the next section I will discuss further how technology and automation may be employed under the auspices of Lean Thinking.

The Lean Deployment in the locations and functions will be where its impact is most tangible. For those who visit those locations, the change in the ways of working and the visualisation of the activities will be significant, as discussed in Chapter 9, although the most exciting element will be the engagement of the people, as they are the ones who will be making the Hoshin, daily management and problem solving activities happen. In Chapter 20 I will cover how we can effectively keep our employees engaged.

It is important that the Lean Leader ensures that both the verticals and horizontals are equally considered in the Lean Transformation and one of their biggest challenges will be that the end-to-end improvements are seductive for most people for a couple of reasons. Firstly they can appear bigger and provide larger step-change improvements than the more incremental change and improvement in the locations and, secondly, and I think crucially, it panders to the belief that others need to change in order to be successful. To explain, in my experience it is uncommon for people to try to do a bad job. If they are disengaged, they may not go that extra mile but they are unlikely to actively make the process fail. In a traditional organisation, when you talk to them about improvements to the processes, they will most often focus on the elements of improvement that others need to make in order that their process can work better, for example:

> *Our quality fall-off rate could be reduced if the designers would do a better job. We could increase sales if the factory could deliver on time. Our customer service would be better if our sales people didn't make silly deals.*

Whilst it is likely that there is some element of truth in what is said, the Lean Leader cannot allow this kind of thinking to be part of the Lean Transformation but must rather engage the people in the functions and the locations to take ownership for their part of the value streams and be accountable for getting their own house in order. At the same time they must reassure and include the team members in the end-to-end improvement activity and ensure that they know that the overall transformational vision is being executed.

Autonomation

As discussed earlier in the chapter the deployment of tools, such as automation and robotics, will only work if we properly involve our people. This is becoming more important in our increasingly technologically enabled world and, if we are to believe recent news reports, many of the jobs currently undertaken by humans will be automated within the next 20 years. In fact, in a report on the BBC website,[2] the figure given was as high as 35%. The site even offers the opportunity to check the likelihood of your job becoming automated.

However, the general concern in the media seems to be in the vein of what is sometimes referred to as the 'Luddite fallacy', whereby the assumption is that the automation of jobs and the technological unemployment associated with it will cause structural unemployment. Therefore the implication is that if 35% of job types are automated, the people in those roles will become permanently unemployed.

Whilst I in no way wish to underplay the impact of any type of redundancy on the people involved, let alone that which is brought about by automation, I do believe that the progression of technological advancement is both inevitable and beneficial to society and that it will, as has been witnessed continually in industrial history, result in a demand for additional and new roles. Just think of the numerous roles that the IT revolution has created, with many of the jobs having been non-existent 20 years ago and, in some cases, even 10 years ago (just think of the role of app developer). However, the real challenge for both society and businesses is in ensuring that both the people entering the workforce from school and those whose roles are automated have the right skills for those new jobs.

Nevertheless, there is a different concern that, whilst not new, I see as increasingly prevalent and contrary to the very Lean Thinking and Lean Leadership that I believe delivers superior customer service and hence business performance. This is the prevalent view of automation as a silver bullet to solve problems and reduce costs, a view that is gaining momentum, especially as the technology becomes more sophisticated, reliable and cheaper across most areas of industry.

If we think about it, fundamentally the leadership of almost all organisations have the same strategic objective, which is to improve their respective enterprise's performance. That is common whether it is a multinational corporation, NGO, government department or a family-run small business. The only differences are in metrics of performance and aspects that they value.

To make this targeted improvement, the organisation needs firstly to understand what its customers value and secondly to improve its capability to deliver that value. That is where automation can play a strong role but, and this is a big but, only when the automation is implemented and deployed in unison with the other key elements of capability, that of i) capable processes and ii) competent and engaged people.

It is in this aspect that organisations often fail to implement automation effectively, as they deploy technological solutions without proper attention to the processes and people development aspects of capability. Furthermore, consideration of customer value is often ignored, with decisions on automation made based upon the 'efficiency' of the value-added portion of the value stream, as opposed to considering the total lead time and hence the amount of waste within the system. This can, and often does, result in value streams that have highly automated processes but long lead times, impacted by a high level of defects, waiting times, over-processing, overproduction (a favourite of automation) and the inherent inventory that it leads to.

This is not to suggest that automation is a bad thing to do, quite the contrary, but it must only be done with an equal attention to people and process development. This approach, where the system of capability is created, is what in Lean Terms has been named Autonomation, a hybrid term formed from the words automation and autonomy. It has a history that dates back at least to the 'intelligent loom' developed by Sakichi Toyoda at the end of the 19th century, which was able to stop itself when a thread broke, allowing the operator to intervene and solve the problem. It was this approach to, and belief in, Autonomation that has informed the thinking of Toyota since its beginning and enables a key element of the Toyota Production system, Jidoka.

However, Toyota are not the only company to question automation without consideration, as recently Mercedes illustrated the advantage of Autonomation with the assembly line for their new S-Type,3 when they opted to utilise smaller, more flexible robots, working side by side with their team members and with much more focus on the flexibility that people bring in delivering customer value. The S-Type is one of their premium offerings and, as such, they need to be able to offer their customer a plethora of options, which requires that nearly every car going down the line is different in some aspect. This is where human intelligence and flexibility, combined with the consistency and labour-saving attributes of robots, designed into a capable process, provide the capability required to deliver customer value most effectively.

The capability triangle

For automation to truly be automation, the machine or robot must not only be able to reliably and consistently execute the process but must also be able to both detect and solve defects. Very few automation solutions can do this and therefore human intervention is generally required. Where the human aspect is treated as subordinate to the robot, the organisation will be penalised by low effectiveness, delivered as low productivity, service and quality. However, where the automation is clearly positioned as the enabler of the performance of the team members, they will take ownership of the process and deliver the customer value that the enterprise needs.

Whilst my examples might seem to imply that I am referring to the world of manufacturing, this is relevant to any part of the customer value chain or its enabling functions. I was inspired to write this section of the book after attending the Infosys Confluence Conference. The event was held in San Francisco in April 2016, where the theme was 'Zero Distance' and many aspects of automation and robotisation were presented and discussed. Being responsible for my company's partnership with Infosys BPO, I am well aware of the high level of competence that Infosys have in this area and we are jointly working on a number of automation initiatives in the accounting operations processes they support.

Nevertheless, we have learned that the efficacy of automation is only as good as the competence and engagement of our people and the effectiveness of the processes that it supports. We have therefore embarked on our joint Lean Transformation whereby we ensure that all three elements of capability are addressed. This aims to ensure that we adequately adopt the philosophy of Autonomation into our approach.

Getting beyond an automation-led approach to efficiency and instead developing an Autonomation strategy toward operational excellence will take, as always, more time and effort in the planning but will ensure that the performance improvement is significantly higher and far more sustainable. It will ultimately ensure that we continue to live the Lean Leadership Paradigms of long-term focus of purpose, utilising proven and reliable technology, building a culture of stopping to fix problems, standardising tasks and processes and using only reliable technology that serves our people and processes. Above all, it will help in the most important aspect of a Lean-Thinking Organisation, that of respect for people.

When we are able to do this we will ensure that our capability is maximised, delivering operational excellence and rewarding our customers, and hence our business, with a significant improvement in quality, service and cost.

HANSEI

Before moving onto the next chapter, please take a few moments to reflect. When it comes to your own way of working, what are:

1. Your key learning points?

....

....

....

....

2. The changes that you could make?

....

....

....

....

3. Current problems that they would help to solve?

....

....

....

....

PART V
LEADING WITH LEAN

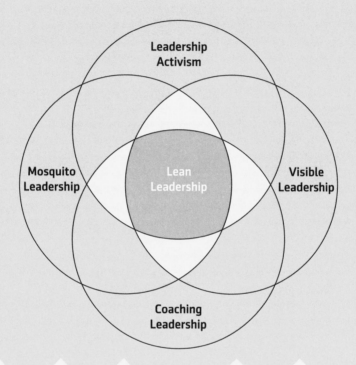

18. MAKING THE NEW WAY OF WORKING THE CULTURE

Being the culture that you want

Earlier in the book (Chapter 11) I presented the beliefs of the Mosquito Leader and one of them, 'I am the culture of my organisation, not the victim of it, and I will never blame it for my failure to deliver or let it prevent me from doing what must be done,' is directly related to the theme of this chapter.

The Lean Leader knows that they must model the behaviours that the organisation has decided it wants in the future and the only way to do that is to truly live them. Let's face it, anything other than genuinely living and breathing the behaviours will be obvious to the team members. If you think about it, it makes sense that we must live as we want things to become, as to do otherwise is to perpetuate the past. The most succinct way I could think of to illustrate this is to say that:

> *The present is the sum of the past and therefore we must live as we want to be, not as we were.*

Whilst the discussion about culture and culture change has increased in significance over the past few years, particularly in relation to the impact of culture on organisational performance, it appears that there is a perception that culture should be directly changed or significantly influenced through culture-change programmes.

This triggered me to take some Hansei (deep reflection) time to consider what this really means in terms of driving, or improving, the performance of a business. While I have my own views on how the performance culture of an organisation may be positively improved, I first wanted to discuss what I consider an insidious symptom of the dialogue around culture, which is for individuals to blame the organisation's culture on their inability to perform at a high level. I'm sure that if you think about it, you will have heard something similar to the following:

> *You know what the culture is like here, we just don't do things that quickly / don't work that way / they just never do what they should / etc.*

We seem to have created a sort of 'culture culture', whereby we assume that we are powerless to oppose the culture of the organisation that we work in and must slavishly behave as it commands. However, what makes up the culture of an organisation? It is surely its people and the sum of their behaviours, the mindsets that those behaviours drive, which in turn creates the culture of the organisation, which in turn influences their behaviours, and so on.

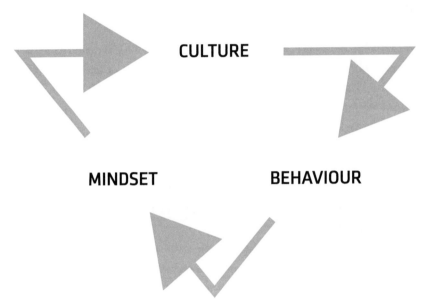

CULTURE

MINDSET   BEHAVIOUR

The culture cycle

Therefore if I, as a member of the team, accept the culture as it is and choose to behave as it influences me to do, then I am part of the sustainment of that culture and, if I simply sit, passively waiting for a culture-change programme to be launched or for senior management to change the culture, then I am simultaneously the victim and the perpetrator of this 'crime against high performance'.

It appears to me that if, instead, we take individual responsibility for doing the right thing, even when we feel that the culture is against us, we can start to move the needle and, as our colleagues see the change, they will be influenced to also make their personal contribution to the change in behaviour. This, of course, requires the employee to be highly engaged and that is why the Lean Leader should take the lead as a role model as they must, by definition, be an engaged employee if they are to lead the Lean Transformation.

I recently read a very interesting book, entitled *Verdraaide Organisaties* (Twisted Organisations), in which the author Wouter Hart[1] has used a similar model to that of Simon

Sinek's 'Why? How? What?' model. However, in his model the inner circle is the purpose of the organisation, the middle ring is the 'real world', the actual environment that we live and work in, and the outer ring is the 'system world', the policies and procedures of the organisation.

In his book Wouter describes how every organisation has all three elements and that the difference between an excellent organisation, with a culture of high performance, and a poorly performing one is the direction of the arrow driving their people's behaviour. If the arrow runs from the inner circle to the outer ring, then the organisation will be working based upon its purpose and meaning and the resulting performance will be high. If, however, the arrow runs from the outside in, the performance will be hindered by a culture of bureaucracy and poor customer experience.

This resonated with my thoughts on this matter and also reinforced my belief that, if we as individuals can take personal ownership of work based upon the purpose of our organisation, we can make the difference. I realise that it takes extra energy to do this but, the reward and sense of liberation can be astounding and together, through our individual action, we can be the culture that we want.

The Lean Leader's mission in making the new way of working a culture is therefore focussed on driving the behavioural change of the organisation; encouraging, reinforcing and requiring that the team members and the leadership consistently repeat the new skills that they have been taught, reminding them of the principles of a Lean-Thinking Organisation until these behaviours become a mindset (a way of thinking) and ultimately a significant part of the culture of the organisation.

This behavioural intervention point is critical and very practically based and contrasts with the more common approach of mindset training. In this approach, the mindsets desired by the organisation are taught to the team members, possibly with the behaviours discussed and described, but without practical reinforcement on an ongoing and consistent basis. The usual result of this approach is people well-versed in the terminology of the principles, mindsets and behaviours required but without well-practised application of them. This will not result in the culture change required by the organisation, although it will create a 'cottage industry' of culture-change professionals.

The Lean Leader must therefore ensure that the culture-change programme is not something separate from the Lean Transformation Programme but is integrated into the Lean Deployment Model. Although basing it on good theory and involving culture-change specialists and HR professionals is beneficial, it must be practically based and simply the outcome of making the deployment of Lean Thinking into the organisation a success.

The problem with problems

Problems are everywhere in life and, in any organisation, the day consists of continuously solving problems. If we want to put a positive spin on it, we can rephrase it and say instead that we have myriad opportunities. However, despite being someone of a generally optimistic demeanour, I prefer to think in terms of problems, as I find that better solutions are delivered when we first focus on what the problem is that needs to be solved.

The problem with problems is that they take time to solve, meaning that every problem that a team or team member spends their time on costs money and detracts from them spending time on other problems. If we look at problems from this perspective, an organisation must therefore do three things excellently if it is to maximise its effectiveness and become world-class:

- Prioritise problems at every level of the organisation.
- Problem solve quickly and effectively.
- Put in place sustainable solutions.

World-class companies do all three really well and by doing so they free up their people's time to focus on achieving more and therefore taking the opportunities that the problems have presented for them. Effective problem solving must therefore become part of the way of working and the culture of the organisation.

At the top level of the business there is the problem of delivering the strategy and achieving the organisation's vision and mission. For example, the core theme of the strategy might be to deliver a certain increase in market share, sales revenue or EBITA.

To achieve the strategy, the organisation needs to determine, with facts, what the problems are that are currently causing the gap between their current state and the desired state. In this example, it could be that their product or service offering is insufficient to meet their customers' needs due to technological, quality, price or delivery gaps; or it could be that they have insufficient geographical coverage for their customers or potential customers.

Perhaps the market is too fragmented, their competitors are stronger than they are in one manner or another or that there are particular barriers to entry of one form or another. There may also be competency gaps that need to be addressed or they may be operationally inadequate and therefore unable to achieve the necessary cost of goods sold or service delivery.

The organisation therefore needs to take the time to truly understand, from the perspective of customer value, what its priority problems are, and their root causes, in order that it may focus its scarce resources on only those solutions that will create the breakthroughs that will deliver the strategic objectives.

The methodology use by the best organisations was covered in Chapter 6: Hoshin Kanri (aka policy deployment) is an approach to problem solving the strategic objectives of an organisation in a highly effective manner. What the approach delivers, when utilised well, is an organisation aligned and focussed on delivering those priorities. This approach, when executed well, avoids the overloading of initiatives and frequent changes in priorities that are common in the majority of organisations.

However, it is not only at the top of the organisation that the prioritisation of problems is essential. At every level of the company problems will be encountered on a daily, if not hourly, basis and we cannot solve them all immediately. Therefore, to drive performance and operational excellence, we will need to solve those ones that, cumulatively, give us the most impact for our resource spend and this requires prioritisation. Doing this is not easy but there are a few tips to help and, if followed, the organisation's team members can learn to apply rapid prioritisation and problem solving:

- Ensure that daily management is in place, (preferably) with leading performance indicators (PIs) and regular team dialogues at a pace most appropriate for the takt of the team. This may be hourly, daily or weekly but must be frequent enough to head off problems rather than react to service failure.
- When the team finds a problem, it must be immediately registered as a concern and an owner determined. Ideally, it will be captured on the 3C (concern, cause and countermeasure) board of the CommCell (communication cell) to ensure that the PDCA cycle is followed and, as Taiichi Ohno said:

No problem found today should take longer than tomorrow to resolve.

- On a shop floor, either in a physical (e.g. a manufacturing line) or a virtual (e.g. a service centre) setting, escalating problems will most likely be via an Andon call by the operative to their direct supervisor at a very short interval, whilst in other environments it could be at the next Communication Cell (daily management) meeting, project review or via a phone call.
- Whichever the method, it must be at an interval sufficiently short for the takt of the process, with the guiding principle being that it must be short enough

to provide the opportunity to solve the problem before any significant delay or customer impact is created.

- The owner's first task is to confirm the concern as a problem statement and determine if it is serious enough to require attention. The time to do this will depend upon the size of the problem but in any case, the owner should follow a similar process to determine the 5W + 1H problem statement with the H (How much of a problem is it?) allowing a decision on whether resources should be spent.

- One common mistake made at this point is to only focus on those problems that are large, that is to say have the biggest potential improvement impact but, naturally, take the most effort. This is a common mistake in organisations where only 'experts' solve problems and normally results in a lot of smaller but cumulatively more impactful problems being left to fester.

- In operationally excellent organisations, everyone solves problems and therefore prioritisation is made along the 'opportunity corridor', with a few large problems being solved via projects, quite a number becoming multiday, cross-functional Kaizen events and a great many problems being solved on a daily basis by the team members through Kaizen (sometimes referred to as 'quick and easy Kaizen' or QEK).

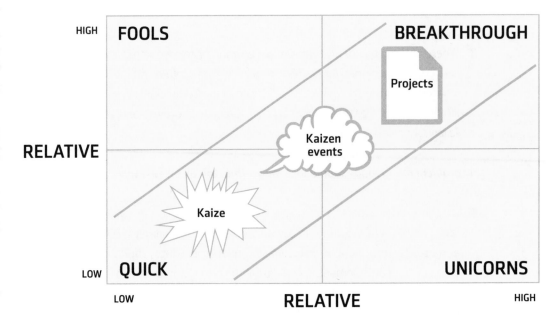

The opportunity corridor

- This inevitably means that most of the problems at the bottom left-hand corner are tackled, as they are quick and easy to solve and therefore the team members themselves will undertake the problem solving.
- One very important caveat to the prioritisation process is that safety-related problems should always jump straight to the top of the list and quality-related issues should be deferential only to safety. A 'safety first, quality always' approach is a prerequisite of excellence and so must be endemic in our problem-solving mindset.

Once the choice has been made of which problems to solve, rigour and discipline are required to solve the problems quickly and effectively but the fact that the time has been taken to prioritise will mean that the assigned team members will have more time to focus on those 'chosen few' instead of being overwhelmed by the 'hopeful many'. Leadership support for the rapid solution of the problems is essential, with the term rapid being relative to the scale of the problem. However, those problems at the bottom left-hand side of the opportunity matrix would be expected to be solved very swiftly, maybe in an hour or so but certainly within a day or two, whilst those at the top right-hand side might take significantly longer and could take several months to completion. Nevertheless, the important thing is that the process of problem solving is as rapid as possible given the problem, rather than slow due to the excessive burden on the team members and the associated waiting time. This is where the leadership play their role. Another critical element in making problem solving the way of working is that the solutions put in place should be sustainable. Again, sustainable is a relative term, as in some cases the solution might be short-term to alleviate the problem whilst a longer-term solution is implemented. This is, in fact, one of the reasons why it is rare to hear the term solution used in many Lean-Thinking organisations, as they prefer the term counter-measure which, by nature, is always temporary, just for varying time periods. You will therefore find short-term and long-term countermeasures in use but never permanent ones, as the problem can always be solved better in the longer term. This is the essence of continuous improvement and a Kaizen culture.

However, rather than being a matter of semantics, the critical element of a countermea-sure is that, regardless of its duration in solving or alleviating the problem, it is controlled and planned. What this means is that, whether it is addressing a root cause or a symp-tom, this is known and chosen and the duration of its control is planned. There is certain-ly no guesswork involved, although there may well be an element of experimentation. This is ultimately what I mean when I talk about a sustainable solution, one that has been based upon true problem solving, with a controlled and planned countermeasure put in place to solve the problem in the best way known and possible at that time.

Rewarding execution, not ideas

At their most positive, ideas are the fuel of innovation and an organisation without ideas is one poor of spirit. Nevertheless, ideas are sometimes used for self-aggrandisement rather than innovation and this can be debilitating to performance, as team members are rewarded for their ideas rather than the delivery of results. This is an environment where highly ambitious ideas of what we should, could or will look like are valued and rewarded above actions that actually deliver more modest results.

What you will observe in an organisation that is operating in this way is that there is a surfeit of ideas that are regularly delivered, often in the form of email but also in very nicely crafted PowerPoint format. However, connected with this are a couple of other symptoms that point toward an organisation of idea mongers rather than innovative problem solvers, namely no formal review system for assessing the actual success of projects or programmes and many ideas directed toward what others should do, rather than what I or we could do.

Referring back to Simon Sinek and his Why, How and What codification, whether it be the Wright Brothers, Apple or an operator on a production line, the idea that they have must be based upon the solution of a problem with meaning, even if that meaning is relatively small in the scheme of things. It must be a problem for which the solution will result in increased value for the customer and, above all, the person with the idea must take ownership for the success of its execution. The Lean Leader must therefore ensure that the organisation focuses on rewarding and recognising those employees who have not only delivered ideas for improvement but have assumed responsibility for their successful implementation.

What sport teaches us about leadership

Like many trainers, teachers and authors I often use sports metaphors as a way of illustrating a learning point. Sport is something that the vast majority of people enjoy, whatever the form or type that it may be, and all sports share with Lean Thinking the elements of respect for people, commitment, engagement, standards (rules of the game), performance metrics and ranking, innovation, continuous improvement and, for many sports, teamwork. We can therefore learn a lot from the metaphor of sport. Rugby in particular is a sport that I think epitomises how we can make Lean Thinking part of our way of working.

In 2015 the Rugby Union World Cup[2] concluded with a fantastic spectacle of a final between the All Blacks (New Zealand) and the Wallabies (Australia), with New Zealand coming out the winners. However, the sport as a whole was the real winner, as this tournament, which happens every four years, continued to grow in its demonstration of the values and ethics that drive its participants, administrators and fans.

So what can we learn from rugby about leadership (and in particular Lean Leadership)?

The most important overarching element is respect for people, with all of the stakeholders (the players, the referee and assistants, support staff, spectators and administrators) demonstrating an enormous respect for each other through their behaviour. It is absolutely amazing to see a 260 lb (120 kg) player, with the adrenalin flowing and only seconds earlier having been embroiled in a maul, being spoken to by the referee and in response simply saying 'Yes Sir' and walking away without argument or obscenity. This respect for both the game and the arbitrator of its rules shows a discipline that is needed in all walks of life and definitely in our leadership roles.

This respect for people flows into many elements of the game, with 'safety first', another key element of leadership, demonstrated in the use of temporary replacement players when head injuries have occurred, preventing a disadvantage from removing a player to provide treatment, combined with solid regulations around concussion, which team medics apply rigorously. The rules of the game are also applied thoroughly to avoid serious injury in what is a very physical and potentially dangerous sport.

Rugby honours its traditions very well and each team brings elements of tradition with it, the most famous, of course, being the All Blacks and their haka. Nelson Mandela used the Rugby World Cup hosted by South Africa, creating national support for their rugby team (the Springboks), as part of his 'healing' of the nation during the 1995 World Cup (which they won 15-12). This became a legend and eventually a Hollywood blockbuster. Honouring the traditions of an organisation for the greater good is an extremely important part of leadership.

I hope that it is becoming clear that rugby can teach us quite a lot about leadership and there are a number of other examples that we can take from the World Cup:

- 'Go to Gemba': It almost goes without saying and seems very obvious, but the leadership of Rugby Teams (including the administrators) do not determine how to drive strategy and problem solve sat in an office or behind a computer screen but by 'going to Gemba'. They understand that they must be at the place where the value is added (the rugby field) while the game is underway to understand what needs to be improved.

- Yokoten learning: The Argentinian team displayed a significant improvement in their performance at this World Cup. One of the drivers of their success was their recent inclusion in the Southern Championship, an annual tournament between Australia, New Zealand and South Africa, in which they now take part. This participation has provided them with the opportunity to continuously improve their game through learning from their competition. Leaders must develop their teams by helping them to learn from best practice and the ideas of others, rather than trying to reinvent the wheel.

- Setting stretching but achievable targets: The Japanese team set themselves the stretching target of winning at least one game during the tournament, something which they hadn't achieved in 24 years. Their head coach (Eddie Jones) did this through a form of policy deployment over the previous couple of years, which included reducing their reliance on players born overseas (the Rugby Union World Cup allows participation in national teams under residency rules). In the end they won three games, including a shock defeat of South Africa. Leaders need to set stretching targets and participate in the achievement of those targets, in a way that breaks through barriers and reaches further than originally thought possible.

- Learning from Failure: As mentioned above, South Africa suffered a shock defeat by Japan in their first group game. However, as all good teams should, led by their head coach Heyneke Meyer, they worked through their learning from this defeat and made it to the semi-finals.

- Focus on changing culture through behavioural intervention: The Australian team, despite being beaten in the final, have made a spectacular transformation from the team that was under the shadow of a precarious culture only a year before. I won't repeat their issues here but their head coach (Michael Cheika) has turned around the team's performance by instilling the discipline of behaviour that was required of a world-class team. Every leader must work with their teams to define the behavioural standards that will determine the culture of the organisation.

- The team is bigger than the individual: While there are certainly stars in each of the teams, the language used by the players and coaches and the actions of the players on the field of play make it clear that the players see themselves as subservient to the team as a whole. This form of camaraderie must be nurtured by a leader, as 'superstar' team members do not, ultimately, deliver the sustainable high performance that we require.

■ Rewarding practice: Carter, the New Zealand fly-half, is a model example of a player whose consummate professionalism, in terms of rigorous practice, delivers game-winning moments. However, in Rugby Union, many of the players are amateurs and still demonstrate a high level of commitment to practice. A leader must ensure that this commitment to practising their particular area of expertise is valued through support and focus, including allowing access to training, coaching and professional networks.

■ Everyone is a leader: To take Carter once again as an example, during the World Cup Final Australia were making a comeback and looking like they might turn the game around and win. However, Carter took a decision to attempt a drop-kick, which was successful and took the wind out of the sails of the Wallabies, giving New Zealand a renewed impetus from which they went on to a convincing win. Enabling the organisation to support leadership by all is critical to creating a high-performance organisation.

There are many examples of great leadership, but I believe that the game of Rugby Union truly epitomises the type of leadership that creates a high-performance organisation and drives operational excellence. If we can take inspiration from this credo of respect, integrity and discipline in our business, I believe that we will be much better off.

HANSEI

Before moving onto the next chapter, please take a few moments to reflect.
When it comes to your own way of working, what are:

1. Your key learning points?

2. The changes that you could make?

3. Current problems that they would help to solve?

19. LEAN: A LIFETIME OF JOURNEYS

A journey must have a destination

A Lean Transformation is often referred to as a journey and I understand why, as it is a learning experience, there are many challenges to overcome along the way and the outcome is not always predictable. However, whilst a journey without a destination might be exciting on a gap year or for the USS Enterprise,[1] for most organisations, especially those that are in business with a clear purpose (whether that be a profit or not–for–profit organisation) the journey must have a destination.

In fact without a destination, which is essentially the company's long-term objectives, which should be described in its strategy and deployed via Hoshin Kanri, the Lean Transformation will be detached from the business and perceived as something separate from the overall activity of the organisation. Despite my emphasis on the importance of establishing the Why of the Lean Transformation, the essential difference between traditional and Lean Thinking to delivering high performance in an enterprise is not the Why of the organisation or What it wants to achieve but How it will achieve its objectives. The Lean Leader is therefore obliged to ensure that the Lean Transformation is clearly focussed on delivering the goals and objectives of the organisation and that it will do it better in terms of both business results and people engagement than other possible approaches.

This doesn't mean that the journey never ends, as the very definition of continuous improvement is that the end is never reached and that performance can always be improved. The Lean Deployment Model, for example one such as the VIRAL model, must therefore be designed in such a way that a long-term destination is set but that it is subsequently updated as the organisation gets close. It is therefore essential that there must always be a destination and, as we get close to it, we set our sights further afield and continue on our travels.

There are multiple journeys

The most rewarding aspect of driving a Lean Transformation is that, just as the organisation has a destination but never reaches it, the Lean Leader will travel, but never really complete, multiple journeys. This in itself requires a Lean mindset, as the Lean Leader will have to accept three undeniable truths:

1. They will reach a point at which they will have done as much as they can for the organisation or a part thereof and need to hand over the baton to someone else.
2. Further improvement will always be possible and their legacy will be one that will (hopefully) be improved.
3. There will always be new journeys for them to join and to determine a destination for.

What this means is that the Lean Leader needs to be able to 'let go' of what they've done, as further development and continuous improvement will require a new set of eyes and a new perspective. This is a truism for life in general but is especially applicable for a Lean Transformation and can be difficult to accept, particularly where there has been a lot of success. However, the Lean Leader must accept that, just as they asked the organisation's employees to embrace change, so must they.

The Lean Leader must therefore see their goal in life as being to make their role redundant, as whilst they are needed, they have not succeeded. In essence, the less they are required, the more successful they have been and this can be a difficult experience for the human psyche and one of the reasons why firefighting is such a prevalent form of management.

This is a challenging aspect both of finding a Lean Leader and of being one, as they must be people who are comfortable as explorers, willing to go into the unknown and break new ground, while others are either passively or actively resistant. However, metaphorically speaking, once the village has been established, there are other people who are better placed to govern and further develop it, so the explorer must move on to find pastures new. This is the beginning of their new journey.

Making yourself redundant

In my role heading up the team that is tasked with guiding Philips Accounting Operations' journey to operational excellence, I often use my Hansei time to consider whether I am adding sufficient value for the customer. However, figuring out exactly who my customer is and ultimately what that value is can be a complicated discussion. My job is certainly not to make things more complicated than they already are, so I consider that my job is a waste or non-value-added (NVA), plain and simple and, as with all NVA in the value stream, it must be removed.

The team that I currently lead is responsible for managing the key elements of operational excellence within accounting operations:

- Partnership development and contract management with our BPO partner
- Quality management
- Data analytics
- Our Lean Transformation

These elements, and the drive for operational excellence, are key to the delivery of our strategy. I therefore believe that my team are currently fulfilling essential roles, and I must say that they're all doing a splendid job. Nevertheless, if I apply the Lean Thinking that I must, we have a duty to our organisation and our customers to consider these activities as, at best, currently essential NVA and in the long term as simply NVA and must aim to simplify, reduce and remove as much of this work as possible. This means that the need for the roles must be minimised, embedding the activities as far as possible into the standard work and the daily management of our operational teams.

At this stage I feel obliged to clarify that I'm talking about the roles of my team and not the people. People are never a waste or NVA but the roles, or part thereof, that they play might be. However, as a measure of the team's success we must reach the point, as soon as is sustainably possible, whereby our services in these roles are no longer required, as we need the operational team members to be just as skilled, if not more so, than we are in the utilisation of Lean Thinking in their domain. At this point my team members should move into either another transformation or into an operational leadership role. By thinking in this way, I hope that my team and I can adopt the mindset that, everywhere that our intervention is required, there must be competency gaps in the operational team that we are having to fill and that, by definition, this is wasteful (NVA) activity. If we can develop those competencies in the organisation and ultimately remove the need for our intervention, we can increase the value added significantly. Similarly for my role, if I'm successful in coaching and developing my people, the first step of success must be to remove the need for my role, as the team should develop into an autonomous, self-directed team, co-developing their plans with the business and executing them with excellence.

I realise that it is uncomfortable to think of our roles in this way but a lot of us do fulfil roles that, in the medium to long term, must be considered NVA and it is my view that we should embrace this fact and be the architect of the eradication of the role. This should not be seen as a negative thing, as if we do it well we will increase the fulfilment that we derive from the role and have a significantly positive impact on our organisation, developing ourselves in competencies such as Lean Thinking, coaching, change management and leadership. This will be a platform for our next career step, helping us to develop a career path delivering more value added for the customer.

Returning to the discussion of my own role in particular, whichever way I look at it ultimately the need for my role must be removed if we are to consider our transformation to a Lean-Thinking, operationally excellent organisation a success and I must make it a personal mission to develop our organisation and our people to the point that my role is defunct.

Simply put, my job is to make my job redundant. If I'm successful, it will result in the organisation no longer needing me in that capacity and I'll be moving onto my next Lean journey.

It's not déjà vu if you love it

I was once asked during a job interview whether taking on another Lean Transformation role would be boring, as it would be very similar to my previous role. My answer was to ask the interviewer whether they thought that Lionel Messi[2] became bored playing his next European Championship game or whether Serena Williams[3] was bored playing at Wimbledon once again.

Just as with sports, the same rules, equipment or even location do not need to mean that the game is the same and hence boring. Each time there will be a different opponent (business challenge), some development in technology (IT, automation) and new players coming through the ranks (new team members) and, provided that the player (the Lean Leader) focuses on the objectives, applies their experience and continues to learn, boredom will never set in.

To use the oft-quoted cliché, they say that if you love what you do you'll never work a day in your life and I truly believe that this is how it works for the Lean Leader, as they do not get their fulfilment from the strike of the football or the stroke of the tennis racquet but through the scoring of the goal or the winning of the point. The Lean Leader is therefore motivated by the results and outcome of the Lean Transformation with engaged people, happier customers, more success and better business results than ever before. This means that they will stay motivated no matter how many times they begin the Lean Journey.

In my own case I've been privileged to have begun the Lean Journey several times within the same organisation, despite still being on the same journey that I began over eight years ago. What I mean by this is that, for most medium to large organisations, there are multiple value streams and many sectors, divisions, business groups, etc., so whilst I am on a journey with the enterprise overall, I have also instigated or been involved in a number of the sub-journeys within the business.

This is exciting and the learning opportunity is a privilege that very few people experience in their careers, seeing multiple functions and most parts of the value stream. The Lean Leader is therefore in something of a unique position vis-à-vis a 'regular' role and can leverage this to develop an appreciation of the overall business dynamic that only a few of their colleagues will share.

The key message from this chapter is that the Lean Leader ought to be someone who understands and believes in business and operational excellence as the outcome that they strive for and utilises the Lean Journey to deliver the Lean Thinking into the organisation that will enable it. They must love what they do and the engaged people, delighted customers and superior business results that it delivers and will never consider the start of a new journey as a backward step but rather as an exciting opportunity to apply and increase their experience and learning within a new team.

HANSEI

Before moving onto the next chapter, please take a few moments to reflect.
When it comes to your own way of working, what are:

1. Your key learning points?

....

....

....

....

2. The changes that you could make?

....

....

....

....

3. Current problems that they would help to solve?

....

....

....

....

20. STAMINA, STAMINA, STAMINA

Being the lone violinist

Throughout the book I have described the numerous differences between a Lean-Thinking and a traditionally thinking organisation. However, if I had to choose just one thing that I believe truly differentiates the two, it would be stamina, the ability to keep going long-term, even when it becomes difficult or there are other interesting alternatives to seduce the leadership.

No matter how well the organisation deploys Lean Thinking and drives its Lean Transformation, it will take a significant amount of time to become a truly Lean Organisation and most organisations have been on the journey for 10 or more years before they feel confident enough to say that they are at a level close to world-class. This is not to say that the benefits from the Lean Transformation won't be gained earlier than this; in fact most organisations start to see the benefits within only a few months of the start of the transformation, but this is precisely the risk, as complacency often sets in and a 'declaration of victory' comes too soon. This was discussed earlier in terms of Kotter's change leadership approach and is a likely root cause of failure for a Lean Transformation.

The organisations that have truly become Lean Thinkers, such as Toyota, Danaher, Virginia Mason and others, have managed to maintain a long-term vision of excellence and have maintained the stamina to keep doing what they know needs to be done. Short-term performance challenges haven't been allowed to derail their programmes as they have progressed and new leaders have not been permitted to 'make their mark' by introducing a new initiative that they have chosen to sponsor. Instead, new leaders have been required to learn and utilise the organisation's Lean Business System to achieve their results and have been educated in this way of working and thinking.

It is inevitable that there will be at least one point, and possibly multiple points, in every Lean Leader's stewardship of the Lean Transformation when this challenge will present itself. Whatever the reason may be; for example, a change of leadership, external factors such as market changes, or new ownership; the organisation will either actively or passively begin to move away from the Lean Deployment approach and it is the duty of the Lean Leader to prevent this from happening.

This is a tough situation to be in and many people capitulate in this situation, either shrinking back into the new role that the shift of focus creates, moving into a new role in the organisation or leaving for pastures new. This is understandable, as it will be lonely to stand and fight this organisational loss of strategic focus when it feels like the whole of the organisation is moving away from them. Nevertheless, this is when the Lean Leader must take up their position as the lone violinist, this seemingly lone crusader for Lean Thinking, struggling against the re-emergence of traditional short-term thinking in the enterprise.

However, it is unlikely that the Lean Leader is completely alone and, if they persist in Leading with Lean and the Leadership styles required, at a minimum they will be able to form a band of lean resistance fighters across the business. This stamina, the unwillingness to stop doing what is right for the organisation in the face of short-term initiatives and programmes, is what will ensure that the organisation's Lean Transformation prospers and will ensure the longevity required to gain the world-class performance that is sought.

Keeping employees employed

A key component of organisational stamina is gaining the engagement of the workforce and the subsequent higher retention of employees. Employee engagement, the art of keeping those employees whom you want to keep, can be a challenge, particularly in the emerging and developing countries but it is also a challenge in the developed world. The biggest issue is that a lot of the time those who leave are those whom you would most like to retain, being those able to find pastures new most easily.

One of the most common reasons for leaving a job is a disengaging environment, which means that, if we can find the right approach to engage our team members, we can increase our retention and make a significant contribution to becoming a high-performance organisation.

To explain the approach a bit further, consider the Retention Triangle:

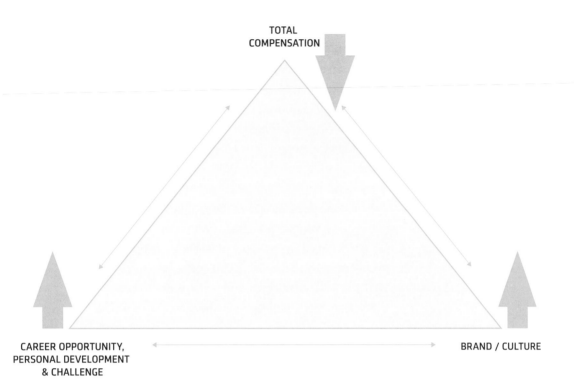

TOTAL
COMPENSATION

CAREER OPPORTUNITY,
PERSONAL DEVELOPMENT
& CHALLENGE

BRAND / CULTURE

The retention triangle

The retention triangle is used as a model for the three key elements of the retention of employees:

1. Brand and culture:

The brand of your organisation can engender pride and loyalty in your employees, particularly if it is one which is well known in the local community for the quality of its products or service, good community citizenship, environmental responsibility, charitable endeavours, or other such things. If this is underpinned by a strong vision, mission and values, and it permeates the organisational culture, your employees will find it more difficult to leave and, those that do will give feedback on their less positive experiences at other employers in comparison to yours.

It is therefore essential that a well-structured and excellently executed communication strategy and plan are in place to inform the employees and also to engage in dialogue with them around the organisation's brand and culture. It is also extremely important that this is not just seen as the responsibility of the HR department but as the accountability of all leadership as the ambassadors of the company and its culture.

Critical to the communication strategy will be a well thought-out reward and recognition system, with a big emphasis on the recognition part. The power of recognition is significant, whether it be a simple thank you from the boss or an award during a town hall meeting or conference. Rewards are a nice complement to this recognition but should be relatively small in monetary value and preferably a nice token or memorial of the recognition. Where possible, team-based reward schemes are particularly good, as they can support and embolden the autonomous work groups that we would like to create within our organisation.

However, recognition and praise will not work in a culture of low overall engagement and so cannot be the only part of the equation and will need to be integral to the overall cultural approach. A culture of performance management, with open dialogues and clear prioritisation, is required to facilitate an environment where our people's talent can shine and they are able to understand how they contribute to business success and are motivated to do so. Leaders must facilitate this culture of performance through coaching and by getting out of their team members' way when they are doing the work.

2. **Career opportunity, personal development and challenge:**
Career opportunity, personal development and challenge are elements of their job that most employees want and this is not simply the cliché of promotion to the top of the organisation but can be as simple as, for example, an operator who would like to become a team leader or a procurement engineer who wants to work in marketing. Providing these types of opportunity for existing employees and avoiding the 'familiarity breeds contempt' trap, which often results in external recruitment, will create an environment whereby employees see opportunity and interest in the organisation and a bright future.

> *CFO asks CEO: 'What happens if we invest in developing our people and*
> *then they leave us?'*
> *CEO: 'What happens if we don't, and they stay?'*

Coupling this with personal development opportunities, through a mixture of formal training, leadership and peer coaching, and on-the-job training, will help team members to grow their talent and feel in control of their own development, an autonomy for which most of us yearn.

As a final point, we must ensure that our team members feel challenged in their role. This should not be confused with overloading them, or giving them tasks for which they are inadequately equipped, but instead providing them with stretch goals and assignments and ensuring that there is a culture of performance whereby they know their targets and how they can meet them, problem solve deviations from the targets and have the support to succeed.

3. **Total compensation:**

This final element is the one which usually gains the most attention, as it is ultimately the reason why most of us work for an organisation; to earn the money required to facilitate our lives. This is why work is sometimes referred to as our 'livelihood' or 'gainful employment'. However, it is this element that has been proven to be the least effective in terms of motivation of employees in the long run.

The compensation in its totality, when all components such as salary, pension, bonuses, allowances, etc. are considered, must be competitive in the market place. However, if the first two elements of the Retention Triangle are well executed, it need not be a package that is competitive at the highest end of the market scale comparable to similar organisations, as the investment in career opportunity, brand and culture will provide a higher retention factor than compensation could account for.

Many organisations take advantage of this and are able to offer lower overall compensation as a result of the collateral elements that a job offer brings and will, in fact, welcome the positive attrition that occurs as people leave to pursue higher offers. The combination of employee engagement and a business system that quickly inducts, trains and develops team members will ensure that their overall employment costs are lower and their people more effective than their traditionally managed competitors.

If we embrace the retention model, we can utilise it as a way to drive employee engagement and to increase organisational capability through the development of our people. This can boost recruitment, as employees become ambassadors of the organisation and word of mouth permeates, describing the positive elements of a career. Of course, the employees that are being developed will be highly marketable and 'good attrition' will occur but, with a mature attitude to their departure, thanking them for their service and leaving the door open for a future return, the culture will only be enhanced and our organisation's reputation in the marketplace bolstered further.

Employee retention need not be an art form anymore but can be an integral part of Lean Leadership and both the catalyst, and outcome of, the creation of a high-performance organisation.

Making history

In his much read LinkedIn article Jeff Haden[1] describes 10 beliefs that he attributes to those people who are extremely successful in what they do. Whilst reading them I could very quickly see how these 10 beliefs were applicable to the Lean Leader and certainly the last three of them, which are related to the theme of this chapter, the need for stamina.

For completeness, the 10 beliefs that Haden attributes to the successful are:

1. Success was only inevitable with hindsight.
2. I can choose for myself.
3. I am not self-serving; I am a servant.
4. I may not be first ...but I can always be last.
5. I will do one thing every day that no-one else is willing to do.
6. I don't build networks; I build real connections.
7. Strategy is important; but execution is everything.
8. Real leadership is measured in years, not moments.
9. Hard work comes first; payoff comes later.
10. I can make history - and I will.

The reader may themselves note that all 10 can be assigned to one or more elements of Lean Leadership and those last three describe really well the need for the Lean Leader to have the vision, endurance and the patience to see the transformation of their organisation through. In fact, as has hopefully become patently obvious within this book, the essence of the Lean Leader is their long-term vision, hard work and desire to leave a legacy that is their defining feature.

Lean Leadership is truly measured in years, not moments. Although there is a need to ensure that wins are continually achieved and celebrated to maintain the organisation's motivation, in line with Kotter's Change Leadership model, the Lean Leader must equally maintain their vision of the long-term goal and not be seduced by the desire for high-profile successes that would negatively impact the long term. This can be difficult, as many of their leaders will be crying out for this and others will be willing to participate for the short-term satisfaction and exposure that it brings. However, the Lean Leader will maintain their true north and the fidelity to the strategic goals that they committed to. Allied to this will be the hard work required to achieve the strategic objectives, which will be a significant investment and again require faith in the ultimate vision. Leading with Lean is Living Lean and requires that the Lean Leader values the importance of doing things properly and invests the energy to make it happen. They will be continuously coaching their team members and colleagues to do things according to the Lean paradigms and will need to invest a great deal of effort in doing this, which will be a long-term commitment, generally with a long-term payback horizon.

Nevertheless, the Lean Leader who has been prepared to commit and live these beliefs will earn the reward of a legacy, perhaps not at the level of some of the great leaders of human history but nevertheless, in their own modest way, a legacy in the transformation that they have helped to lead in their organisation. This is the Lean Leader's way of making history.

HANSEI

Before moving onto the next chapter, please take a few moments to reflect.
When it comes to your own way of working, what are:

1. Your key learning points?

2. The changes that you could make?

3. Current problems that they would help to solve?

21. LEADING WITH LEAN

Being a yardstick of quality

Steve Jobs once said:

> *Be a yardstick of quality. Some people aren't used to an environment where excellence is expected.*

A quality mindset will only pervade the organisation when the Leadership actively models the behaviour. Only by living the approach to quality that they desire can leaders truly drive the change to a culture of quality and, if we are to deliver a truly excellent organisation, we need to lead in a way that enables it. The proposition of this book is that Lean Leadership is the best way to achieve this, provided that it is practised authentically, consistently and in the long term, regardless of business pressures.

The quality mindset is central to Lean Thinking and embodies a much wider definition of quality than is generally understood, meaning that quality must be delivered by everyone in everything that they do. This should not be confused with an organisation trying to be the best in class in everything that they do, as it may be that some elements of their offering are specified at a 'good enough' level, as they are not differentiators of value for the customer. However, the defined specification must be delivered right first time and the quality mindset applied equally to that of those differentiating elements of the value stream.

Delivering operational and business excellence is not something that can be achieved by controlling the outputs of processes, which is why so many companies fail to achieve this level of performance. Rather, it is the sum of each step of the processes within the value stream and therefore everything that we do matters.

Manufacturing companies can generally see this in their product value streams more easily than service organisations can in their service value stream, as the physical nature of a product means that quality defects within processes often are visible. Nevertheless, the vast majority of manufacturers still allow poor quality in their process steps and rely on catching issues as the end of the line.

Fortunately, Toyota and the majority of the automotive industry led the way for manufacturers several years ago and many manufacturers have made big steps toward Lean Manufacturing. Nevertheless, even in those manufacturing companies that have made their production a showcase of Lean thinking, other parts of their organisation, such as their design, marketing, sales and finance functions still leave a lot to desire in terms of the application of Lean Thinking.

Some service organisations have in the last few years also made good progress in their transformation through Lean Thinking. Earlier in the book I highlighted Virginia Mason as one such organisation. I have also visited financial organisations such as ABN AMRO[1] and Euroclear[2], who have made good progress and industries as diverse as insurance, utilities, railways and construction.

The four leadership styles required to achieve Lean Leadership are complementary and, whilst each on its own is already positive, their cumulative impact is much larger than the sum of the individual parts. In fact, if one or more of them is overlooked or omitted, there will be a deleterious effect on the overall efficacy of the leadership and so the leader must ensure that they focus effectively on building their competence in all four styles.

In fact, the most positive approach is where leadership teams are able to agree that they will all live and breathe Lean Leadership and are able to support and challenge each other along their journey. This is the approach proposed, where a formalised Lean Excellence Model ensures a unified and collective method for the deployment of Lean Thinking.

The Lean Leadership model

Bringing together the leadership styles required to achieve Lean Leadership in a Venn diagram, it is clear that it can only be achieved when all four styles are running in harmony.

The Lean Leadership Venn diagram

If one or more are missing there will be consequences for the impact of the Leadership Style within the organisation:

- Without Leadership Activism the essential element of modelling and leading by example will be absent.
- Without Visible Leadership the employees will not see what the leader is doing and they will become detached from the teams.
- Without Mosquito Leadership the leader's impact on the organisation will be limited to their span of control, which will usually, even in the case of senior leaders, be quite small.
- Without Coaching Leadership, the leadership will appear directive and the results will be unsustainable.

Where Lean Leadership is practised, learnt and applied, employee engagement will bloom and the organisation's performance thrive, bringing benefits for everyone; customer, employee, leader and shareholder.

This book was intended to equip the aspiring Lean Leader with the thinking needed to deliver operational excellence in their organisation and help them through the long, challenging Lean Journeys that they will lead. Their musical exploits as the lone violinist and experiences living the four leadership styles will hopefully be made a little easier as a result of the advice and I wish the reader great success for the future.

Leading with Lean - A conclusion

Writing this book has enabled me to share with you what has become part of my every-day way of working. I have aimed to demystify what can sometimes appear to be overly complicated to those early in their Lean Journey.

The book is probably a little unconventional in its storytelling and format but expresses Lean Thinking and Lean Leadership in the way that I have experienced, taught and lived it. It's not easy to be the lone violinist and it isn't a natural thing to truly challenge the paradigms of an organisation but it is necessary if real change is to be achieved and operational excellence attained. I do hope that this book inspires others to take this path, one that I have been treading now for many years.

I began the book with the metaphor of the lone violinist and I want to end it with a plea, to take the road less travelled and lead your organisation in its transformation, regardless of your position in it, as I can attest that it only takes one person to change the culture of an organisation.

HANSEI

Before finishing the book, please take a few moments to reflect on your overall reading experience. When it comes to your own way of working, what are:

1. Your key learning points?

2. The changes that you could make?

3. Current problems that they would help to solve?

NOTES

Chapter 1 Introduction

1. 'Pearls before Breakfast', *Washington Post*, April 8, 2007:
    https://www.washingtonpost.com/lifestyle/magazine/pearls-before-breakfast-
    can-one-of-the-nations-great-musicians-cut-through-the-fog-of-a-dc-rush-hour-
    lets-find-out/2014/09/23/8a6d46da-4331-11e4-b47c-f5889e061e5f_story.html
2. The Toyota Mindset: *The Ten Commandments of Taiichi Ohno*, Author:
    Wakamatsu, Yoshihito, Publisher: Enna Inc. (5 October 2009), ISBN-10: 1926537114
    Gallup 2013 Employee Engagement Survey; Gallup.com
    Harvard Business Review 2013; The Impact of Employee Engagement on
    Performance
3. *Lean Thinking*, Author: Womack and Jones, Publisher: Simon and Schuster (2003),
    ISBN-13: 978-0-7432-3164-0
4. Hansei (反省, self-reflection) is a central idea in Japanese culture, meaning to
    acknowledge one's own mistake and to pledge improvement. This is similar to
    the German proverb *Selbsterkenntnis ist der erste Schritt zur Besserung*, where the
    closest translation to English would be 'Self-awareness is the first step to
    improvement.' Source: Wikipedia.com

Part I - Planning to Lead

Chapter 2 What is Lean?

1. © Shingo Institute, Utah State University, 3521 Old Main Hill, Logan, Utah 84322,
    http://www.shingo.org
2. Collin McCloughlin, '5 Myths About Lean That Are Holding You Back',
    LinkedIn.com, Feb 1, 2016.
3. *Lean Thinking*, Author: Womack and Jones, Publisher: Simon and Schuster (2003),
    ISBN-13: 978-0-7432-3164-0

Chapter 3 Beginning the Change

1. Start with Why TED Talk, September 2009
2. *Start with Why*, Author: Simon Sinek, Publisher: Portfolio (2011), ISBN-13: 978-1591846444
3. Net Promoter or Net Promoter Score (NPS) is a management tool that can be used to gauge the loyalty of a firm's customer relationships. It serves as an alternative to traditional customer satisfaction research and claims to be correlated with revenue growth. Source: Wikipedia.com
4. Stakeholder analysis in conflict resolution, project management, and business administration, is the process of identifying the individuals or groups that are likely to affect or be affected by a proposed action, and sorting them according to their impact on the action and the impact the action will have on them. This information is used to assess how the interests of those stakeholders should be addressed in a project plan, policy, programme, or other action. Stakeholder analysis is a key part of stakeholder management. A stakeholder analysis of an issue consists of weighing and balancing all of the competing demands on a firm by each of those who have a claim on it, in order to arrive at the firm's obligation in a particular case. A stakeholder analysis does not preclude the interests of some stakeholders overriding the interests of the other stakeholders affected, but it ensures that all affected will be considered. Stakeholder analysis is frequently used during the preparation phase of a project to assess the attitudes of the stakeholders regarding the potential changes. Stakeholder analysis can be done once or on a regular basis to track changes in stakeholder attitudes over time. Source: Wikipedia.com
5. PDCA (plan–do–check–act or plan–do–check–adjust) is an iterative four-step management method used in business for the control and continuous improvement of processes and products. It is also known as the Deming circle/cycle/wheel, Shewhart cycle, control circle/cycle, or plan–do–study–act (PDSA). Another version of this PDCA cycle is OPDCA. The added O stands for observation or as some versions say, 'Grasp the current condition.' This emphasis on observation and current condition has currency with Lean Manufacturing / Toyota Production System literature. Source: Wikipedia.com
6. The Philips Community is a Business-Specific Social Media platform provided by SocialCast. It provides the opportunity to share user generated content through groups that may be formed by users based upon specific interests such as a subject matter, function, geography or other relevant connection.

7. The number of members was over 2500 as of 1 February 2016 before the split of Royal Philips into two wholly owned but separately operated companies focussing on the health technology and lighting business sectors. Since the removal of the Philips Lighting employees from the Philips Community, the *ContinuousImprovement@Philips group* membership has reduced to around 1770 members as of 22 May 2016.

8. John Kotter is a *New York Times* bestselling author and is considered by many to be the authority on change leadership. He promotes his thought leadership through his company Kotter International and is an international speaker and Harvard professor.

9. Kotter's e-book 8 *steps to accelerate change in 2015* is available from the KotterInternational.com.

10. Omron Corporation (オムロン株式会社, Omuron Kabushiki-gaisha) is an electronics company based in Kyoto, Japan. Omron's primary business is the manufacture and sale of automation components, equipment and systems, but it is generally known for medical equipment such as digital thermometers, blood pressure monitors and nebulizers. Omron developed the world's first electronic ticket gate, which was named an IEEE Milestone in 2007, and was one of the first manufacturers of automated teller machines (ATM) with magnetic stripe card readers. Source: Wikipedia.com

Chapter 4 The Importance of Conscious Incompetence

1. The Dunning-Kruger effect is a cognitive bias in which relatively unskilled persons suffer illusory superiority, mistakenly assessing their ability to be much higher than it really is. Dunning and Kruger attributed this bias to a metacognitive inability of the unskilled to recognise their own ineptitude and evaluate their own ability accurately. Their research also suggests corollaries: highly skilled individuals may underestimate their relative competence and may erroneously assume that tasks which are easy for them are also easy for others. The bias was first experimentally observed by David Dunning and Justin Kruger of Cornell University in 1999. They postulated that the effect is the result of internal illusion in the unskilled, and external misperception in the skilled: 'The miscalibration of the incompetent stems from an error about the self, whereas the miscalibration of the highly competent stems from an error about others.' Source: Wikipedia.com

2. How to improve your Hiring Practices by Christine Lagorio-Chafkin, 1 April 2010, www.inc.com

3.   Tony Robbins is an entrepreneur, best-selling author, philanthropist and America's number one life and business strategist. A recognised authority on the psychology of leadership, negotiations and organisational turnaround, he has served as an advisor to leaders around the world for more than 38 years. https://www.tonyrobbins.com/

Chapter 5 Building the Lean Transformation Model

1.   Honeywell invents and manufactures technologies that address some of the world's most critical challenges around energy, safety, security, productivity and global urbanisation. According to their website they are uniquely positioned to blend physical products with software to support connected systems that improve homes, buildings, factories, utilities, vehicles and aircraft, and that enable a safer, more comfortable and more productive world. Their solutions enhance the quality of life of people around the globe and create new markets and even new industries. www.honeywell.com

2.   Danaher is a global science and technology innovator committed to helping customers solve complex challenges and improving quality of life around the world. Their family of world-class brands have an unparalleled leadership position in some of the world's demanding and attractive industries, and their technologies address a range of global needs. www.danaher.com

3.   Virginia Mason is recognised as one of the USA's best healthcare facilities. Virginia Mason's network of primary and speciality care medical centres and Virginia Mason Hospital and Seattle Medical Center offer superior treatment outcomes. www.virginiamason.org

4.   Porsche are a leading manufacturer of performance cars and began their Lean Journey in the early 1990s as a result of significant financial underperformance precipitated by a proliferation of models and poor quality. www.porsche.com

5.   The Unipart Group is a leading provider of manufacturing, logistics and consultancy services. Why this combination? They believe that these areas of expertise provide the skills, technologies and markets for continued growth. Their proprietary business system, The Unipart Way, enables them to build a unique range of capabilities to deliver productivity improvement and innovation for all customers. At the heart of The Unipart Way is a commitment to engage employees at every level of the organisation and to provide people with the skills and knowledge to be great at whatever they do. www.unipart.com

6.   The change curve is based on a model originally developed in the 1960s by

Elisabeth Kubler-Ross to explain the grieving process. Since then it has been widely utilised as a method of helping people understand their reactions to significant change or upheaval. Kubler-Ross proposed that a terminally ill patient would progress through five stages of grief when informed of their illness. She further proposed that this model could be applied to any dramatic life-changing situation and, by the 1980s, the change curve was a firm fixture in change management circles. The curve, and its associated emotions, can be used to predict how performance is likely to be affected by the announcement and subsequent implementation of a significant change.

7.   The purpose of Lean Accounting is to support the lean enterprise as a business strategy. It seeks to move from traditional accounting methods to a system that measures and motivates excellent business practices in the lean enterprise. Source: Wikipedia.com

8.   The Philips Avent Baby Products Factory in the UK won the 2014 World-Class Manufacturer Award at the UK Manufacturer of the Year Awards. www.themanufacturer.com. The Philips Shaving Factory in the Netherlands was the Dutch finalist for the INSEAD European Industrial Excellence awards in 2015. www.insead.edu

Part II - Learning to Lead

Chapter 6 Hoshin Kanri

1.   Source: Marakon Associates/Economist Intelligence Unit, Kaplan and Norton, Harvard Business Report

2.   *Change Without Pain: How Managers Can Overcome Initiative Overload, Organizational Chaos, and Employee Burnout*, Author: Eric Abrahamson, Publisher: Harvard Business School Press (2004), ISBN-13: 978-157851827

3.   A3 is a structured problem-solving and continuous-improvement approach, first employed at Toyota and typically used by lean-manufacturing practitioners. It provides a simple and strict approach systematically leading towards problem solving over structured approaches. A3 leads towards problem solving over the structure, placed on an ISO - ISO A3 single sheet of paper. This is where the process got its name. A3 is also known as SPS, which stands for systematic problem solving. The process is based on the principles of Deming's PDCA

(plan-do-check-act). Source: Wikipedia.com

4. Leader Standard Work involves walking the Gemba (the place where value is added), observing abnormalities, asking questions, and supporting people in the improvement process.

5. The target amount of time for an executive to spend on strategy is around 70% of their time. Based on a 40-hour week over 46 weeks per year this is equivalent to 107 hours per month.

Chapter 7 Leadership Activism

1. *The Lean Turnaround: How Business Leaders Use Lean Principles to Create Value and Transform Their Company*, Author: Art Byrne, Publisher: McGraw-Hill Education (2012), ISBN-13: 978-0071800679

2. John J Oliver, OBE, is the former CEO of Leyland Trucks and an Activist Leader who has applied simple, low-cost approaches to leadership resulting in bottom-line benefits via 'radical' employee engagement. John states that despite the positive publicity about engagement over the past twenty years and the extensive research into its substantial benefits, take-up by businesses is exceedingly low.

3. Gary S. Kaplan, MD, FACP, FACMPE, FACPE, has served as chairman and CEO of the Virginia Mason Health System in Seattle since 2000. He is also a practising internal medicine physician at Virginia Mason. www.virginiamason.org/ceo

4. Virginia Mason has received a number of recognised quality awards over the past eight years, including being one of only two recipients of the Leapfrog Top Hospitals of the Decade award. www.virginiamason.org/QualityAwardsRecognition

Chapter 8 Discipline as a Competitive Advantage

1. Emanuel James 'Jim' Rohn (17 September 1930 - 5 December 2009) was an American entrepreneur, author and motivational speaker. www.jimrohn.com

2. Peter Ferdinand Drucker, (19 November 1909 – 11 November 2005) was an Austrian-born American management consultant, educator, and author, whose writings contributed to the philosophical and practical foundations of the modern business corporation. He was also a leader in the development of management education, he invented the concept known as management by objectives and self-control, and he has been described as 'the founder of modern

management'. Source: Wikipedia.com

3.   Lieutenant General Frank Kearney retired on 1 January 2012 from the United States Army after 35 ½ years of service. His final active duty assignment was Deputy Director for Strategic Operational Planning at the National Counter Terrorism Centre in Washington DC. General Kearney now serves as the President of his own consulting company, Inside-Solutions-LLC, focusing on leader development in organisations and is a partner in and co-founder of Willowdale Services LLC, which invests in and develops small businesses and works to employ veterans.

4.   *Focus: The Hidden Driver of Excellence*, Author: Daniel Goleman, Publisher: Bloomsbury Publishing (2013), ISBN-13: 978-1408829110

Chapter 9 Visible Leadership

1.   Kanban Development is a method for managing knowledge work with an emphasis on just-in-time delivery while not overloading the team members. This approach presents all participants with a full view of the process from task definition to delivery to a customer. Team members pull work from a queue. Kanban in the context of software development can mean a visual process-management system that tells employees what to produce, when to produce it, and how much to produce - inspired by the Toyota Production System and by Lean Manufacturing. Source: Wikipedia.com

2.   *The Lean Turnaround: How Business Leaders Use Lean Principles to Create Value and Transform Their Company*, Author: Art Byrne, Publisher: McGraw-Hill Education (2012), ISBN-13: 978-0071800679

Part III - Leading at Scale

Chapter 10 Learning from Success

1.   Peter Michael Senge (born 1947) is an American systems scientist who is a senior lecturer at the MIT Sloan School of Management, co-faculty at the New England Complex Systems Institute, and the founder of the Society for Organizational Learning. He is known as the author of the book *The Fifth Discipline: The Art and Practice of the Learning Organization* (1990, rev. 2006).

Chapter 11 Going Viral - Mosquito Leadership

1.   Socialcast is an Enterprise Social Media host provider that can be customised for an organisation's internal use. www.socialcast.com

Chapter 12 Coaching Leadership

1.   The situational leadership theory (or situational leadership model) is a leadership theory developed by Paul Hersey, professor and author of the book *The Situational Leader*, and Ken Blanchard, leadership trainer and author of *The One Minute Manager*, while working on the first edition of *Management of Organizational Behaviour*. The theory was first introduced as the 'life-cycle theory of leadership'. During the mid-1970s, the 'life-cycle theory of leadership' was renamed 'situational leadership theory'. Source: Wikipedia.com

2.   *Toyota Kata: Managing People for Improvement, Adaptiveness and Superior Results*, Author: Mike Rother, Publisher: McGraw-Hill Education (2009), ISBN-13: 978-0071635233

Chapter 13 The Business Excellence Competition

1.   As of 1 February 2016 Royal Philips split into two wholly owned but separately operated companies focussing on the health technology and lighting business sectors.

2.   Yokoten is a process for sharing learning laterally across an organization. It entails copying and improving on Kaizen ideas that work. You can think of Yokoten as 'horizontal deployment' or 'sideways expansion'. The corresponding image is one of ideas unfolding across an organisation. Yokoten is horizontal and peer-to-peer, with the expectation that people go see for themselves and learn how another area did Kaizen and then improve on those Kaizen ideas in the application to their local problems. It's not a vertical, top-down requirement to 'copy exactly'. Nor is it a 'best-practices' or 'benchmarking' approach, or as some organisations refer to a 'lift-and-shift' model. Rather, it is a process where people are encouraged to go see for themselves, and return to their own area to add their own wisdom and ideas to the knowledge they gained. Source: www.leanblog.org by Al Norval.

3.   *The Toyota Way: 14 Management Principles from the World's Greatest Manufacturer*, Author: Jeffrey Liker, Publisher: McGraw-Hill Education, ISBN-13: 978-0071392310

Part IV - Leading Excellence

Chapter 14 Creating the Lean Enterprise

1.   Start with Why TED Talk, September 2009

Chapter 15 Breaking the Mediocrity Barrier

1.   The Lean Turnaround: How Business Leaders Use Lean Principles to Create Value and Transform Their Company, Author: Art Byrne, Publisher: McGraw-Hill Education (2012), ISBN-13: 978-0071800679

Chapter 16 Making Business Excellence Excellent

1.   In his article in the Lean Management Journal, titled 'Developing Leaders at Toyota', Jeffrey Liker talked about the importance of prioritisation and focus, and how a lack of them causes leadership failure. https://the-lmj.com/2012/08/developing-leaders-at-toyota/

Chapter 17 Reconciling the Value Stream with Local Autonomy

1.   *Lean Thinking*, Author: Womack and Jones, Publisher: Simon and Schuster (2003), ISBN-13: 978-0-7432-3164-0

2.   In an article on the BBC website on 11 September 2015, it was stated that about 35% of current jobs in the UK are at high risk of computerisation over the following 20 years, according to a study by researchers at Oxford University and Deloitte. http://www.bbc.co.uk/news/technology-34066941

3.   In an article in Bloomberg on 25 February 2016, entitled 'Mercedes boots robots from the production line', it was explained that human beings, along with small robots, provided greater flexibility: http://www.bloomberg.com/news/articles/2016-02-25/why-mercedes-is-halting-robots-reign-on-the-production-line

Part V - Leading with Lean

Chapter 18 Making the New Way of Working the Culture

1. *Verdraaide organisaties*, Author: Wouter Hart, Publisher: Vakmedianet (2015), ISBN-13: 9789013105735

2. The Rugby World Cup is a men's Rugby Union tournament contested every four years between the top international teams. The tournament was first held in 1987, when it was co-hosted by New Zealand and Australia. New Zealand are the current champions, having defeated Australia in the final of the 2015 tournament in England. The winners are awarded the William Webb Ellis Cup, named after William Webb Ellis, the Rugby School pupil who — according to a popular legend — invented rugby by picking up the ball during a football game. Four countries have won the trophy; New Zealand have won it three times, two teams have won twice, Australia and South Africa, while England have won it once. Source: www.wikipedia.com

Chapter 19 Lean: A Lifetime of Journeys

1. The Enterprise or USS Enterprise (often referred to as the 'Starship Enterprise') is the name of several fictional spacecraft, some of which are the main craft and setting for various television series and films in the Star Trek science fiction franchise. Source: www.wikipedia.com

2. Lionel Andrés 'Leo' Messi (born 24 June 1987) is an Argentine professional footballer who plays as a forward for Spanish club Barcelona and the Argentina national team. He is often considered the best player in the world and is rated by many in the sport as the greatest of all time. Messi is the only football player in history to win the FIFA World Player of the Year/FIFA Ballon d'Or five times, four of which he won consecutively, and the first player to win three European Golden Shoes. Source: www.wikipedia.com

3. Serena Jameka Williams (born 26 September 1981) is an American professional tennis player, who is ranked number one in women's singles tennis. The Women's Tennis Association (WTA) has ranked her world number one in singles on six separate occasions. She became the world number one for the first time on 8 July 2002, and achieved this ranking for the sixth time on 18 February 2013. She

is the reigning champion of the French Open, Wimbledon and Olympic women's singles and doubles. Williams is regarded by most commentators and sports writers as the greatest female tennis player of all time. Source: www.wikipedia.com

Chapter 20 Stamina, Stamina, Stamina

1. Jeff Haden learned much of what he knows about management as he worked his way up the printing business from forklift driver to manager of a 250-employee book plant. Everything else he knows, he has picked up from ghostwriting books for some of the smartest CEOs he knows in business. He has written more than 30 non-fiction books, including four business and investing titles that reached number one on Amazon's bestseller list. He'd tell you which ones, but then he'd have to kill you. Source: www.uk.businessinsider.com

Chapter 21 Leading with Lean

1. ABN AMRO is the third largest bank in the Netherlands, headquartered in Amsterdam. www.abnamro.nl/en
2. Euroclear is a post-trade settlement bank, headquartered in Brussels, Belgium. www.euroclear.com

GLOSSARY OF LEAN TERMS

Throughout the book I have used a number of Lean terms, many of them Japanese and, as I mentioned in Chapter 9, I try to use them only where they can help to truly differentiate between their Lean intent and the local language interpretation.

In this glossary I have tried to list a number of common Lean Terms and their meaning. However, I also recommend visiting the Lean Production website for a more extensive glossary at http://leanproduction.com/lean-glossary.html.

WORD OR PHRASE	PRONUNCIATION (non-standard, ad hoc approach)	DEFINITION
ANDON	And On	A visual signal, typically a light mounted on a machine or line to indicate a potential problem or work stoppage
GEMBA	Gem Ba	Gemba is a Japanese word meaning 'actual place', or the place where you work to create value. In manufacturing this is the factory. In each industry the Gemba will be a different place.
GENCHI GENBUTSU	Gen Chee Gen Boo Tsoo ('Gen' as in 'go' not 'general')	Japanese for 'actual place, actual thing' indicating the habit to 'go see' to gain the facts and solve problems based on facts ('Gen' as in 'go' not 'general')
HEIJUNKA	Hay June Kah	Production smoothing; creating a build sequence that is determined by SKU average demand
HOSHIN KANRI	Hoe Shin Kan Ree	A method of policy deployment and strategic decision making that focuses and aligns the organisation on a few vital 'breakthrough' improvements. The objectives and means to achieve the objectives are cascaded down through the entire organisation using a series of linked matrices. The process is self-correcting and encourages organisational learning and continuous improvement of the planning process itself.
JIDOKA	Jid Oak A	Japanese term for transferring human intelligence to a machine through automatic stopping upon detection of errors

KAIKAKU	Ky Kak Koo	Radical improvements or reform that affect the future value stream. Often these are changes in business practices of business systems. The Kaikaku experience is a tour of world-class companies that have already been through a radical improvement programme and have implemented Lean Operating Systems. The experience is designed to offer support, encouragement and inspiration to the businesses about to deploy Lean Thinking.
KAIZEN	Kai Zen	A combination of two Japanese words Kai (change) and Zen (good). A Kaizen follows a PDCA cycle of Exposing a Problem, determining the root cause, implementing a solution, standardising and confirming success.
KAMISHIBAI	Cam E She Buy	The Kamishibai board is a visual management tool for use by senior management team members to confirm that standard work is being undertaken by staff and to maintain standard work discipline. In the same way that supervisors and line managers use an hourly production status board to confirm that the production targets are being met, Kamishibai boards are used for weekly, monthly and even quarterly audits of standard work elements.
KANBAN	Kahn Bahn	A Japanese word for 'sign', Kanbans are typically a re-order card or other method of triggering the pull system based on actual usage of material. Kanbans are attached to the actual product, at the point of use. Kanbans are cards that have information about the parts (name, part number, quantity, source, destination, etc.) but carts, boxes, and electronic signals are also used. Squares painted on the floor to indicate storage or incoming areas are frequently, but mistakenly, referred to as Kanbans.
TAKT	Tact	The word TAKT is German but is widely used in Japan and is the customer demand stated in units of time.
YOKOTEN	Yoko Ten	Horizontal deployment, copying and expanding good Kaizen ideas to other areas

ACKNOWLEDGEMENTS

Writing this book reached into the depths of my professional experiences and, when thinking about those people whose influences have helped me to reach this point, I concluded that it would be impossible to create an exhaustive list.

I consider myself fortunate to have worked for a number of managers of differing backgrounds and from each I've learned about different aspects of Leadership. I've also been lucky enough to have worked for companies that have given me the opportunity to travel and work globally and that have provided the experience of working with some great colleagues. This has led to seeing different perspectives and cultural diversities, from which my own view of the world has expanded greatly. Through these experiences in my career I learnt the importance of being data-driven in my decision making and how to focus on what really matters in an environment of chaos. I learnt what being people-focussed really means and how the best business results are achieved when we develop our people and give them the freedom to deliver.

I am grateful to those many managers and colleagues who have had a positive influence on my career and hope that when reading the book they have recognised their contribution.

This is my first book and it couldn't have been professionally published without the support of Vakmedianet, so I would like to thank Freek Talsma, Laurens Molegraaf, Neeltje de Kroon and the rest of the staff there for their support in editing and publishing *Leading with Lean*.

However, my most sincere appreciation must be reserved for my mother and father Shirley and Jim, my daughters, Megan and Emily, and especially my Wife, Laura, without whom my passion, determination and enthusiasm wouldn't be so great.

ABOUT THE AUTHOR

Philip Holt is Head of Operational Excellence and Accounting Operations at Philips, and explains exactly what his model of Lean Leadership is, how we can learn to apply it and how you can convince the workplace never to settle for anything less than excellence. We also learn how to redefine our leadership style and how to identify and eliminate wasteful activities within the company. This way you can recognize, realize and retain the ideal state. In *Leading with Lean*, Philip Holt shows us the best ways to arrange a high-performance organization, and gives us simple tools and insights for each leader to aspire to greatness, for themselves and for their teams.

Philip Holt is currently Head of Operational Excellence and Accounting Operations at Philips and a member of the advisory board of the Operational Excellence Society. He studied at Manchester Metropolitan University, the University of Pennsylvania (Wharton School) and the University of Warwick. He worked for the Gillette Company before joining Philips, where he has built up a magnificent reputation on Lean practices and advice. By combining Japanese methods with European and American business processes, he has a keen eye for the waste within organizations and the opportunities for cultural change through employee engagement. Philip is a regular speaker at Lean, Six Sigma and Operational Excellence Conferences.